MANAGING HEALTH AND WELLBEING IN THE PUBLIC SECTOR

As governments throughout the world experience increasing fiscal challenges, the pressures on public sectors to streamline services and harness technological advances is unprecedented. Many have undergone huge budgetary cuts as a result, but what are the effects of this intense organisational change on such a large and varied workforce? And how can managers within the public sector meet the challenge of delivering services whilst maintaining the health and wellbeing of staff tasked with carrying out the work?

Managing Health and Wellbeing in the Public Sector: A Guide to Best Practice is the ideal companion for any manager in these challenging times. Exploring the realities of working in the public sector, and those factors which can add meaning and purpose to working life, the book provides managers with a practical toolkit for creating the best working environment, as well as nurturing resilience and motivation within their staff.

Written by two authors with a lifetime of experience in the field, the book also examines why promoting occupational health and wellbeing is beneficial to organisations, drawing on a wealth of international research to support this argument. It concludes with a series of case studies in which an international range of public sector managers discuss initiatives they have implemented, and how successful they have been.

This book is the ideal companion for any manager working in the public sector. It will also be instructive reading for students and researchers of occupational or organisational psychology, as well as HRM.

Dr Ian Hesketh is a serving police officer, currently working at the College of Policing in the UK. Ian has a PhD and an MBA from Lancaster University Management School, and he is a Chartered Manager, Fellow of the Chartered Management Institute, and a Member of the Society for Education and Training.

Professor Sir Cary L. Cooper, CBE is the 50th Anniversary Professor of Organizational Psychology and Health at the ALLIANCE Manchester Business School, University of Manchester, President of the CIPD, President of the British Academy of Management, President of RELATE, and President of the Institute of Welfare. He is a Companion of the Chartered Management Institute and one of only a few UK Fellows of the (American) Academy of Management.

MANAGING HEALTH AND WELLBEING IN THE PUBLIC SECTOR

A Guide to Best Practice

Dr Ian Hesketh and
Professor Sir Cary L. Cooper

Routledge
Taylor & Francis Group

LONDON AND NEW YORK

First published 2018
by Routledge
2 Park Square, Milton Park, Abingdon, Oxon OX14 4RN

and by Routledge
711 Third Avenue, New York, NY 10017

Routledge is an imprint of the Taylor & Francis Group, an informa business

© 2018 Ian Hesketh and Cary Cooper

British Library Cataloguing in Publication Data
A catalogue record for this book is available from the British Library

Library of Congress Cataloging in Publication Data
A catalog record for this book has been requested

ISBN: 978-1-138-92919-7 (hbk)
ISBN: 978-1-138-92920-3 (pbk)
ISBN: 978-1-315-68134-4 (ebk)

Typeset in Bembo
by Keystroke, Neville Lodge, Tettenhall, Wolverhampton

Printed in the United Kingdom
by Henry Ling Limited

CONTENTS

FIGURES AND TABLES

Figures

Table

THE AUTHORS

Professor Sir Cary L. Cooper, CBE

Cary L. Cooper is the author and editor of more than 125 books and is one of Britain's most quoted business gurus. He is the 50th Anniversary Professor of Organizational Psychology and Health at the ALLIANCE Manchester Business School, University of Manchester. He is also a founding President of the British Academy of Management, a Companion of the Chartered Management Institute and one of only a few UK Fellows of the (American) Academy of Management, past President of the British Association of Counselling and Psychotherapy and President of RELATE. He was the Founding Editor of the *Journal of Organizational Behaviour*, former Editor of the scholarly journal *Stress and Health* and is the Editor (with Professor Chris Argyris of Harvard Business School and Professor Bill Starbuck of New York University as Associate Editors) of the *Blackwell Encyclopaedia of Management*, and the Editor-in-Chief of its third edition, now the *Wiley-Blackwell Encyclopaedia of Management*. He has been an adviser to the World Health Organization, ILO and the EU in the field of occupational health research and wellbeing, was Chair of the Global Agenda Council on Chronic Disease of the World Economic Forum (2009–2010) and is former Chair of the Academy of Social Sciences (comprising 47 learned societies in the social sciences and 90,000 members). He was awarded the CBE by the Queen in 2001 for his contributions to organisational health and safety, and in 2014 he was awarded a knighthood for his contribution to the social sciences. In 2014 and 2015 he was voted the most influential thinker in HR. The award, nominated by members of the HR community, recognised his contribution working with businesses in the field of health and wellbeing.

Dr Ian Hesketh

Ian Hesketh is a serving police officer within Lancashire Constabulary, currently seconded as the Senior Policy Adviser for Wellbeing at the College of Policing. During a long and distinguished policing career he has carried out a number of specialist operational roles, including in the Armed Response Unit, Policing Partnerships and the Mounted Branch. He has also worked on secondments with the United Nations in Bosnia and Herzegovina and with the OSCE in Kosovo. Ian also consults as a UK subject expert for the EU accession programme in Serbia. Ian has a PhD and MBA from Lancaster University Management School, Dip Mgt and Cert Ed from the University of Central Lancashire. He is a Chartered Manager, Fellow of the Chartered Management Institute and holds Qualified Teaching, Learning and Skills (QTLS) status with the Institute for Learning. In 2011 his article on 'Transformational Leadership during Change' was voted one of the top five management articles of the year by the CMI. His current research interests are centred on wellbeing, in the context of policing in the UK. Most recently he has introduced the term *Leaveism* to describe a lacuna in thinking around sickness absence and workload overload. Ian is married with two young children.

FOREWORD

Dame Carol Black

In what might be seen as a fuller expression of corporate responsibility, many organisations are concerned to promote and safeguard the health and wellbeing of their employees beyond their responsibilities as set out in legislation.

Most ill health among working-age people is not a result of risks incurred in the workplace. Rather it is a consequence of medical and psychosocial factors over which employers have little control. But there are common circumstances in which employers are in a position both to help safeguard and promote better health and wellbeing among employees who are fit and well, and to give support to those who are not so fit and especially those whose employment might be threatened by ill health or disability.

The conditions of work, where most people spend the greater part of their wakeful lives, even if not directly causal, greatly influence employee wellbeing. And often those working conditions are crucial in enabling people who are not well or are on sickness absence to maintain or resume productive work. Indeed the case is strong that it is in the interests of a business to make this possible.

The Health and Safety Executive has produced admirable guidance on meeting legal obligations to fulfil the duty of care. The guidance contained in this book reaches further. It is for staff of any discipline whose responsibilities and actions might have an impact on the health, particularly the mental health, and wellbeing of employees.

The book explores changes in what were once called industrial relations. Among them are those that have become the necessary response to demographic change, the pressures of the working environment and economic reality.

The guidance is founded on accumulated best practice and informed by the experience of senior people in the public services sector, in the UK and internationally. It offers a broad range of opinion and experience, and gives many examples of actions that have been taken, with clear pointers to what needs to be done, to illustrate which actions enhance workplace wellbeing.

The commitment to support employee health and wellbeing is also a factor in securing engagement and with it improved performance and quality of product or service. These are core issues, nowhere more important than in public services. In the NHS, for example, the wellbeing of staff has a direct impact on the safety and quality of patient care.

This guidance is not of the kind to be adopted and implemented by rote. It signals the need for changed attitudes, capabilities and education and training among those managing employees, to enable them to work in an environment that allows them to sustain and improve their health and wellbeing in the workforce of tomorrow.

INTRODUCTION

Generally speaking, most people set out to have a meaningful and purposeful life. Sometimes things happen that interfere or stand in the way of this, so-called 'life events'. However, we will skip around this for now and concentrate on the day-to-day, or what we may describe as the *drip-drip-drip* of everyday life that can cause people to fall out of favour with even themselves, dependent on some of the notions we will introduce in this book. The vast majority of us will spend a very high percentage of the waking hours of our adult lives at work – estimates suggest as much as 30% of our entire life, or 110,000 hours if that helps? Therefore it makes perfect sense that if work can be meaningful and purposeful, one may have, well, 'cracked it!'

Throughout this book we will return to meaning and purpose, as we believe that, above all, these two 'life-objectives' impact most heavily when it comes to drawing purpose from our working life. The focus of this book is the public sector, and meaning and purpose are probably more pronounced in the public sector, as there is, generally speaking, more of an internal impetus driving workers to give greater levels of effort towards a public need, a call to public good or vocation at the very least. This is set against a backdrop of personal drive, ambition to succeed and financial reward. This final point, financial reward, is probably less pronounced in public service, as the majority in the employment of their government are unlikely to be attracted by huge levels of pay, although we concede this is occasionally contentious. However, although many of these things are intertwined, we propose meaning and purpose trump all, these being the major tenets of wellbeing in public sector working life, and the ones, if managed correctly, that should deliver significant gains.

With many publications currently exploiting the relatively vogue world of wellbeing, this book will concentrate on what it means in the ever-changing world of public sector management, whose boundaries seemingly grow more blurred by the day. This fast-paced change appears to be leaving leaders in public sector organisations with the quandary of establishing what is best practice exactly, and how to implement it effectively, sustainably, and with accountability to the public purse?

One of the peculiarities of public service management is the strong reliance on workers' sense of psychological contract, and the notion that when this is high, meaning and purpose are also high. This, in turn, results in high levels of discretionary effort. It could be argued that one of the key differences between public and private service management is that reliance on high levels of discretionary effort from the workforce in public service. The private sector, it seems, has far more robust approaches to dealing with low levels of discretionary effort that are simply not available to their public sector counterparts. We will unpick why that may be so later in the book. Nevertheless, it seems that public sector work is still very popular across all sections of society, where the draw of serving the public realm remains a strong psychological driver, despite some of the significant challenges faced. There is also a train of thought suggesting this challenge is precisely why some are attracted to the public sphere, being attracted to the mission impossible!

So, how do we successfully manage and make meaningful improvements in such an environment? We hope to provide some, but by no means all, of the answers in this book. Survey after survey tells us that the 'things' in the workplace that obstruct our life ambition are not always drawn out of operational necessity, and very often are just the result of what amounts to poor or uncaring management. As the book unfolds, we proceed to unpack what some of these 'things' may be, but it is safe to say at this point that some are tangible and others take on more of a phenomenological guise that one may struggle to explain rationally, although we will try.

Although there are many publications that discuss this subject matter, this book takes a contemporary look at wellbeing, with a clear focus on the public sector. Apart from the authors' own considerable research in the field, the book will draw on both UK and selected international research, such as the Australian policing study (Jakubauskas and Wright, 2012), Spanish workers study (Schaufeli and Bakker, 2004), Danish hospital workers study (Suadicani et al., 2014), Finnish leavers study (Kivimäki et al., 2003) and the seminal works on positive psychology and happiness in the US (Seligman, 2011; Diener and Biswas-Diener, 2008). In this book we seek to bridge the gap between theory and practice by taking a bird's-eye view of the common issues that have a profound effect on the modern-day public sector workforce: issues such as changing attitudes towards work and the workplace, motivating employees through improved wellbeing, self-belief, job satisfaction and the effective management of change.

Bridging the gap between theory and practice has been a life's work for many, and we hope that this book will go some way to narrowing the gap. The aim of the book is to attempt to bring the science to life and, by using working examples, to illustrate how these theories play out in practice, and what practitioners can also do to bring evidence to the fore. The previous paragraph typifies the academic explanation of theoretical principles in written form. We suggest that this is not an easy read for the majority of practitioners. For example, the broken text, highlighting original authorship, seems to spoil the written flow and can distract the reader from the message. Many explain this as just being 'academics showing off', so we will try to help the flow of the book by a more fluid approach to writing, hopefully allowing the reader to pick up the key points of our message while having a positive experience, i.e. enjoying the read. So, given that you have probably decided by now whether to put this book down or read on, we will further explain the premise.

Though written and set in the UK public sector, this book will be useful to professionals and students alike, all those with an interest in the fascinating subject of workplace wellbeing globally. The book proposes that wellbeing is very much an area for enormous improvement, and that managers and leaders can create an improved workplace environment by paying attention to what is actually going on for employees, by being sensitive and attentive to their needs, and by ensuring work has both meaning and purpose. One may see close proximity to the literature on mindfulness here, and we will include those elements as we progress. Clearly people have a choice as to how much effort they put into their work, and this book suggests that strong connections to the workplace, high levels of engagement and ethical practices can and do lead to optimum performance. We suggest this is born out of an inner commitment to the work in hand, and hopefully motivated by a will and willingness to serve the public. These are very personal phenomena, and people very often have periods of deep reflection about what work means to them.

This deep reflection is considered good for public service motivation (PSM), and we sometimes hear of workers being driven to public service through an engrained focus on this alone, almost unconscious to what else is happening around them. This can especially be seen in emergency service workers, and the oft-used suggestion that they are running towards situations that many are desperately seeking to run away from: incidents of catastrophe or human suffering, burning buildings, road collisions, violent individuals, and so on. We suggest this provides a good lens to view public service management from, where clearly there may be better fiscally rewarded jobs out there, but not so in relation to emotional reward? We may caveat that with the exception of charity related work, but again we may suggest this is related closer to public than private sector employ?

Traditionally books have delivered a diagnosis and then may follow with a prescription. Within this book we deal with all elements that impact on working life, some that can be controlled and others which clearly cannot, such as life events or accidents. Even though these cannot be meaningfully foreseen or anticipated, nevertheless they are going to occur, so there are steps that people can take in preparation. In response to this we devote considerable time to talking about resilience in this book, and things people can learn that help mitigate the effects of these unfortunate life events. Research has shown that resilience training can be an effective means of preparing for adversity, which unfortunately is inevitable.

If you lead people, this is even more pertinent to your duties as a people manager, and if you are reading this book it shows that you, at the very least, wish to know more about workplace wellbeing. It may be you are just a little curious, or it may be you wish to do something more formal, such as creating and documenting a wellbeing strategy? This book will help with both of those goals, and we know that great leaders are almost always equipped with great people skills; arguably that is what makes them great leaders? However, as we will expand on later in this book, the role of the leader in wellbeing is as contested as ever. What is good for one may not be the same experience for another, and we will probe why this may be so. More importantly, we will tell you what to look for, how to spot the signs, and some ideas about what to do in response.

Technology also plays a huge role, and we now juggle with the challenge of leading remote, virtual, flexi, part-time and often very diverse teams. The other side of the technology transformation represents the changing face of work, with literally millions of tasks being automated at a burgeoning rate. A World Economic Forum study predicted that five million jobs would be lost to robots before 2020 (WEF, 2016). On the upside, there is exponential growth in technology related jobs, designing, programming and applications being amongst these. At a recent presentation, Gian Fulgoni, co-founder and chief executive of comScore.Inc, suggested as little as 2% of big data was being mined, leaving a huge opportunity window for those adept at analysing market data. In many public service environments, the subject of data security, storage, analysis and access is contentious and never far from being tabled on the boardroom agenda.

A final introductory mention should be made of one of the vital components of wellbeing, that of stress. Unfortunately stress itself may not be immediately obvious, as, say, may be an injured limb, a bruise or such. However, all of us carry this around with us every day. Some stress is good for us; it drives and motivates us to perform better. Being labelled the 'health epidemic of the 21st century' according to the World Health Organization, it clearly should not go unconsidered. For example, it can make us weak, insecure, vulnerable to disease, diabetes, cardiovascular complaints and depression, to name just a few consequences. Stress is a big deal; this should be the message you take from this book. It impacts on all of us, every day of our lives. Attempts to understand even the basics will make you a better manager, especially regarding how people perceive work and working life. Whilst some people may get immense pleasure from certain activities or work, the exact same thing may cause others unbearable amounts of stress, some of which may not be visible to the naked eye and require effective management to uncover, understand and address. The ability to identify, recognise, intervene in and manage stress may be the greatest insight you gain from this book. Wellbeing cannot be separated from stress, and neither should it. Stress need not incapacitate, and learning how to cope, being resilient, can help individuals learn about themselves and how they react to both the daily stressors of everyday life and personally catastrophic events, such as the loss of a loved one. This final item is, unfortunately, inevitable for all of us. The impact, however, is not uniform, and again we will examine how various reactions manifest. Further, we will look at the actions of managers, often crucial in assisting the return to some sort of normal state, and acknowledging that things may never be the same for that person again. We will also look, on a more positive note, at eustress, or good stress. This comes through challenge, excitement, good anticipation and feelings of doing good and impacting positively on people's lives, in this case their working lives. Introduced by Hans Selye, who is widely regarded as the founder of stress as a concept to describe being well or good, this again is bringing in notions of meaning and purpose in life.

Having hopefully whetted your appetite, we will now proceed to unpack some of these notions of what wellbeing looks like and contains, and how it can be used in public service management.

Why the public sector?

The book is aimed at managers working primarily in public sector employment globally, but is also applicable to other managers, HR professionals and occupational health workers in the private sector, as well as those engaged on educational courses to do with health and wellbeing at work in whatever capacity. When you consider the crossover, it is easy to see that most of the argument put forward in this book is applicable to both public and private sector alike. The focus is on people, and how they think, feel and behave in relation to work. It may not be a critical factor as to just what that work is; it is rather the attitudes and perceptions of those involved in it that are of greatest concern. Managing these aspects is clearly a key to success, so although targeted at the public sector there is no reason at all why private sector readers should not be able to draw a great deal from the contents of the book.

The reason for choosing the public sector is that it seems to be relatively underexplored in respect of a 'what to do' guide or even a 'how to get started' guide, our own experiences of regularly facing the challenge of these two fundamental questions in the quest to promote workplace wellbeing. With the acceptance of non-financial objectives amongst most executives (and now extending to the US, it seems), a new field of exploration has emerged, with employee wellbeing firmly at the centre.

As authors, we both have a lifetime of experience that we will openly share, hopefully in a manner that makes for a compelling read. We also have aspirations that the content of the book, as well as being a valid source of reference, will be enjoyed by readers, who will draw from it personally. We will explore factors that add meaning and purpose to our working life, using short interviews with senior people in the public service sector, both in the UK and internationally, to illustrate what they are doing, and what needs to be done, and mapping these across to produce practical advice on how to successfully deliver sustainable wellbeing in the workplace. This mixture of research and practitioner voice, we feel, will make for far better understanding for those interested in the field generally, for those studying, and for those acting as practitioners, to further develop their skills and knowledge. What is clear is that there is burgeoning interest in this field in terms of both research and practice. In an ever shrinking, and sometimes virtual, world of work, there is a need for guidance amongst those charged with leading public servants through the rapidly changing world of work in a way that is congruent with the wellbeing of their charges. This is not only the right thing to do in respect of emotional labour; it also makes perfect business sense in terms of productivity and performance in the workplace.

Each chapter of this book will explore the reality of managing today's public sector workforce. In an environment of almost constant financial pressure and enduring organisational change, managers need to call on a deeper skill set to manage their staff. We would argue that wellbeing is at the heart of this deeper skill set, and the management of the future will have mastery over interpersonal skills, including empathy, compassion and kindness. We would suggest that it is unlikely that these conditions will change, and that some managers may experience this status quo throughout their managerial careers.

Structure of the book

The first chapter of this book (Context) sets out the challenge for public services in dealing with the fascinating subject of wellbeing. We examine the political landscape, particularly the challenges of austerity and budgetary cuts. We look at the changing cultural scene that HR practitioners are facing, along with new working methods, the introduction of new technologies and the ever-growing thirst to work harder, longer and faster in the name of performance. We provide a description of what working life may look like beyond 2020, taking into account the rate and pace of change across all sorts of business, and the challenges world events throw into the mix. At the time of writing, and in the space of only a few weeks, we have seen the UK vote to leave the European Union, the terrible atrocities of terrorist attacks in France and the UK, an attempted coup in Turkey and the ongoing elections for the presidency of the USA. All require public servants to take on extra tasks in their daily workloads and as such impact on employee wellbeing. And then there is the not so small matter of managing all these public sector employees. We move on to take a speculative view of what this will look like in 2020 in the concluding part of the first chapter.

Carrying on from the first chapter, Chapter 2 (Why wellbeing, why now?) highlights the importance of getting wellbeing right, providing a rationale in terms of the physical, financial and psychological benefits of having an effective wellbeing approach. One of the most important concepts about wellbeing, that it isn't just the absence of ill health, is explored in detail within this chapter. The Hedonic and Eudaimonic aspects of wellbeing are unpacked, and we detail why meaning and purpose are so important to working life, whatever that looks like or involves. We illustrate what getting wellbeing right may look like for managers and provide a framework around which wellbeing is constructed in an organisation, based on the evidence garnered from research on the subject over many years. The chapter concludes with a section on how to create a business case for wellbeing. This practical example forms part of our attempts to bridge theory and practice gaps, bringing the subject out from the page and into a work setting. The second chapter concludes with a look at how culture impacts on wellbeing, and how wellbeing can also be used as a culture-change instrument, modelling attitudes, perceptions, behaviours and processes. The very nature of looking after people in the workplace may bring about huge changes in the way work is both perceived and delivered. Getting the right 'wellbeing culture' can be quite challenging, and we want to avoid it being seen as 'tales from the tofu bar' if at all possible. Wellbeing should be viewed as positive by all; the signs, symbols, rituals, routines, structures and control systems all require adaptation if wellbeing is to truly embed in an organisation, and this section imparts some crucial information that can help make this a reality.

Chapter 3 (Wellbeing: the fundamentals) gets into the mechanics of wellbeing, and we propose there are three themes that can make a big difference in organisations if they are executed in the right way. These are a focus on personal resilience, good leadership and creating the right workforce environment in which people can experience meaning and purpose in their work. These are areas critical to workplace wellbeing. We look at one of the greatest challenges for the public sector, the ubiquitous leadership approach. Given the plethora of research on the subject, we highlight characteristics that are successful in terms of workforce wellbeing, having the effect of motivating, challenging and receiving high levels of discretionary effort from staff. Our model for wellbeing is well proven, and several pieces of research have been published to strengthen our proposal, including our own that majors on resilience training efficacy. With this in mind, we highlight the need to have an evidence-based approach when implementing workplace strategies, concluding the chapter with a few leadership tips for those charged with the management of wellbeing, as well as those who may be involved in wider human resource management.

Chapter 4 (What research tells us) tracks the history of some of the common components of workplace wellbeing, and we set the scene for what we consider are the four key areas of workplace wellbeing. These are psychological, societal, physiological and financial wellbeing. This chapter also introduces the concept of *leaveism*, a phenomenon we observed, labelled and introduced to the wellbeing landscape in 2011. Leaveism is when employees use allocated time off, such as annual leave entitlements, banked flexi-hours and re-rostered rest days, when they are in fact unwell and may be entitled to take sickness absence. The same term can also refer to working outside contracted hours, including when on holiday or on allocated days off, when an employee is well (fit for work) but overloaded and unable to manage their workload within the contracted hours. These leaveism behaviours are distinct from those categorised as 'absenteeism' or 'presenteeism', opening up a new opportunity to explore notions of abstractions from the workplace that are born out of being unwell (sick) or unfit to perform to the requirements of the particular task because of stressors such as work overload, and where an employee may normally be entitled to time off sick. This overload work may be conducted when the employee is well, but outside contracted (i.e. paid for) hours. The chapter concludes with a speculative piece that identifies some of the challenges around the future workplace and employees' roles in that workplace. This highlights that there are many challenges to come for managers, some of which we do not yet know.

Intriguing though this sounds, it may require many different approaches from those that are common today, but nevertheless focus on employee wellbeing.

Our penultimate chapter (Applying research in your workplace: best praxis) is devoted to how to operationalise wellbeing in the workplace. We look at implementation, monitoring, evaluating and developing workplace wellbeing, utilising tools for each step that people can adapt to evidence their own approach. Perhaps from a practitioner's viewpoint this chapter provides a handbook for wellbeing; we believe it offers a useful, at hand, reference tool in itself.

The final chapter of this book provides fascinating insight into wellbeing in public services, viewed through the lens of those charged with delivering it. Several case studies outline vivid examples of the dos and don'ts of workplace wellbeing in various public sector organisations, such as health, police and local government.

1

CONTEXT

Introduction

The aim of this first chapter is to illustrate how the political and economic landscape is incomparable with that of just five years previously. Although we are both based in the UK, these challenges are faced globally, in equal measure, and our aim is to set out the impact this landscape has on workplace wellbeing. Furthermore, society is changing as a result of globalisation and other factors, leading to changing expectations of public services, declining deference to authority, greater social and economic polarisation within societies, and other factors which place greater demands on all public services. Demand for these services is a reflection of the current society that they serve, so these essential political, economic, social and technological shifts are fundamental to the tasks and roles of public services. They also have significant consequences for the education and training within these services; both up-skilling and reskilling are very often required.

The objectives of the chapter will be to deal with the reality of those changes, and what they mean in practical terms for managers and those charged with providing Human Resource Management (HRM), Learning and Development (L&D) and Occupational Health Services (OHS). We concede there may be various names for these functions throughout organisations, but we do not intend to list the many descriptions here.

Public services have been faced with an imperative to make wholesale changes on an unprecedented scale, to *re-imagine* as one commentator put it (Thornton, 2015). This involves both getting the right outcome for the public this sector serves and taking the employees within the sector on a transformational journey.

The burgeoning interest in social media in the sphere of wellbeing will also be explored, challenging how this both helps and hinders our projections of what working life may look like in 2020 and beyond. We relate our extensive use of social media as a global engagement tool to illustrate future scenarios for the workplace, and how it is both possible and quite probable that this will change radically from the status quo. Digitisation and fiscal pressures bear down heavily on the public sector and have a direct impact on workplace wellbeing, so the question may well be: can we keep up?

Political landscape for public services

The landscape of public sector work is changing quickly and dramatically, and managing the workforce in the current environment has never been more challenging. This management includes a focus on cost effectiveness, cultural changes, the use of technology and the rationalising of estate, and all this whilst remaining accountable to the public and juggling political needs which occasionally conflict with working requirements. For example, in the UK the majority of public sector organisations are experiencing unprecedented budgetary cuts, which demand significant down-sizing in all areas of business. This is at a time when there are radical changes to working practices such as flexible, remote and virtual working aimed at maximising productivity, creating a diverse workforce and championing equality. These elements take their toll on the workforce in ways not yet experienced in the public sector. Alongside this, managers who 'survive' in this new world have the almost impossible task of inspiring and motivating those who remain. Unlike in the private sector, these are not necessarily the people of choice, for a variety of reasons, such as the likelihood of getting equivalent employment elsewhere, being tied into a pension scheme or having domestic responsibilities, such as caring, that restrict their options. This is very often conducted against a backdrop of political change, election campaigning and so on. These considerations don't necessarily impact as hard on private sector organisations, whose direction may not be as politically driven and is more focused on profitability and market share.

Indeed, across the globe we see unprecedented events impacting on public sector workloads, for example the UK referendum result indicating a preference to leave the European Union, and all the planning and extra work (and workforce) that will need to be put in place to facilitate this. Not to mention that the referendum plunged the government political parties into near chaos, with both major UK political parties undertaking radical reform, including the installation of a new prime minister. In France and the UK we have witnessed horrifying scenes of terrorism across the country, with incomparable scenes of murderous acts requiring public service responses at unprecedented levels. In Turkey we have witnessed an attempted coup, plunging that country into a state of tension and public unrest, again causing immense stress and strain on many public services. The presidential elections in the USA have been less than cordial and caused much unrest. Still in the US, there have been numerous police shootings in Dallas, and there is the ongoing problem of marauding gunmen in a variety of US states. The seemingly never ending unrest in the Middle East, the civil war in Syria and the resultant migration crisis facing Europe all require public servants' dedicated attention in serving their respective publics. This work is far from easy and challenges the very heart of public service around the globe. At the time of going to press the UK has also been subject to horrific terrorist attacks in the city of Manchester, in the north of the UK, and on two occasions in the capital, London. These attacks have seen public services, particularly first responders, stretched to their limits. This has effectively forced a rethink about a whole host of issues that impact on the wellbeing of employees and their current working landscape.

Changing face of working life

As we will see, the public now expect to read, hear and see how their money is being spent, and have an expectation that it is done effectively, efficiently, fairly and justly. This brings in to play notions of social responsibility, fair procurement, ethical working practices and wider human rights considerations, largely centred on the workforce. We hear of *legitimacy* in the language of public services. One of the many crossovers we see with the private sector is illustrated in this respect, with blurred boundaries between public and private sector working practices. As we see more outsourcing, shared or integrated services, collaboration, joint ventures and so on, there is an expectation that private outsourced work will adhere to public sector ethical standards. This has caused some consternation, and there are many examples of private contracts being unable to sustain these standards over time, and contracts being handed back to the public sector. One particularly stark example played out in the security contract for the UK London Olympics in 2012.

However, what both the public and private sector share is the notion that there needs to be a strong psychological contract between the employer and employees, and the relationship is better being built on a long-term commitment from both sides to do right by each other. The long term we are referring to here is the length of contract of employment, the term of the relationship. For both to have a healthy psychological contract there needs to be mutual respect and the notion of fairness on both sides. There is also the notion that, as well as being fair, there needs to be good work. We will look deeper into engagement, discretionary effort and work–life integration later in the book, but when we look at the changing face of work, retaining levels of what may be considered good work can be quite challenging. And, as we will see later, as work becomes more technology focused, the boundaries of what is good work can get blurred. What one employee perceives as autonomy and being trusted to get on with the job, working remotely and flexibly, another may view as being isolated, lonely and uncared for, and so one needs to be careful.

A further issue to consider in terms of the changing face of working life is that, with jobs becoming increasingly capable of being carried out virtually, the pool of people able to carry out the work is opened much wider, potentially globally. The consequences of this can be viewed in a number of ways, and although public servants are traditionally drawn from the locality, or at least the same country, this may not be so in the future? Private sector companies have been bold in outsourcing work overseas, to a far cheaper labour market. This seems to have had a wide variety of success, largely dependent on cultural barriers and the ability of the organisation to maintain healthy relations with its customers. This can have what seem to be fairly obvious outcomes, for example the product or service becoming available at a much-reduced cost to the end customer or user. However, issues such as language differences, interpretation, quality of product and so on have driven some organisations to backtrack and return to employing in the locality, or the same country at least.

Kurt Lewin (1890–1947) outlined what is regarded as a fundamental approach to helping organisations through radical change programmes with minimum disruption and the notion of permanence. This is not a new theory, but as it has stood the test of time it would seem there is merit in much of his stance. Lewin floated the notion of workers creating their own goals to improve workplace performance. He effectively had workers researching themselves (participatory action research) and the way they carried out their roles, and advocated work as a 'life-value', congruent with suggestions of meaningful work. Taking an active part in their own work regime appeared to have the effect of linking motivation to action. In the model he developed is a notion of unfreezing, moving to a new paradigm and then refreezing (Lewin, 1947). Incidentally, Lewin carried out research in German textile mills, a wallpaper factory and in America at a pyjama factory (Harwood Plant). What most contemporary public service workers will identify with is the *unfreezing* and *moving* aspect. We would hazard a guess that these days most would not recognise the bit referring to the *refreezing*? And fundamentally herein lies the problem. As tenured, and now mostly democratically elected, governments change across the globe, and technology bears down in more intricate ways, the pace and change of life seem relentless. Yet within this fast-paced paradigm, the human body and its mechanisms to cope have changed very little. What there is, however, is a plethora of advice and guidance indicating, based on our genetic make-up, some assumptions of what our capacity to deal with all this may be. It is then left to us to decide how we process and utilise this information and knowledge in our working lives.

We were fortunate enough to watch Professor Eddie Obeng relate this to an audience a year or two ago at one of the superb 'Good Day at Work' events. With his own particular style he managed to drive it home that there is so much, literally too much, information out there for us to consume, or even process, and therefore we are left with choices. Even within these choices we sometimes have to make choices about choices. By way of example, 20 or so years ago researching for a dissertation would involve hours in a university library hunting down fitting material to include in your thesis. These days, it is a matter of an online search, yielding thousands upon thousands of results that need sifting out, via whatever mechanisms seem appropriate, to get to some sort of list that is small enough to make up a relevant discussion for your work. And even then you could be wide of the mark. Casey described us living and operating in a world of volatility, uncertainty, complexity and ambiguity, the so-called VUCA world (Casey, 2014). Although he was speaking in the context of the US military, this certainly now appears to be an appropriate description of the world faced by public servants. With all this in mind, how do public sector staff cope in the workplace, how do they integrate work and private life, if at all? How does all this change affect health and wellbeing?

Working practices 2020 and beyond

This next section looks to the future and what the impact of contemporary ways of working may be. Will the majority of public service work be done remotely? Is homeworking or remote, virtual and flexible practice going to be the standard way of doing things in the public arena in the future? Rigid clocking on and clocking off, booking worked hours, what are worked hours, when are we at work, what bit of a conversation can be 'booked' as work with all this informality? These are all considerations for future practice. One of the challenges for this future working paradigm may be how we account for time. In public services, how we describe 'the job' may be particularly challenging. Will it be public service, as we know it now, or something entirely different? For example, when the public contact their public services, how will this be done? With the availability of media such as Facetime, Twitter, Snapchat, LinkedIn, Messenger and so on facilitating face to face interaction, will it be done from an office space, from a home setting or whilst on the move? And what will constitute a 'unit of chargeable work'? More issues for service providers come into play around the nature of recruiting the right people for such posts: will this be done in the traditional way, i.e. an advertisement, a selection process and a contract of employment being drawn up and worked to? With the global nature of work, will these people be sited in the home country or overseas? How will employment be regulated? All these questions combine to make it a very interesting future for agile public services, and it may be a little too ambitious to resolve them all in one publication. We can however make some headway!

We could begin by looking at the work of the public sector, as an alternative to the private, although as we have already mentioned the boundaries are becoming increasingly blurred. However, we can still try to think about why people take this (public sector) route into working life. We can say, broadly speaking, that work can be viewed through three lenses. First, it can be seen as a transaction for money. But, in terms of public service, the fiscal rewards have never been on a par with those in the private sector. However, traditionally it has always been viewed as infinitely more secure, so economically minded pragmatists could argue that over a lifetime, in terms of secure regular pay, public service trumps the private sector. This has of late become a somewhat out of fashion view, with public service work now seen as relatively short term compared to what it once was, especially in relation to pensions and the ubiquitous gold clock. The final salary pension scheme has all but disappeared in the UK landscape, in both public and private sector; for example, not a single FTSE 100 company now offers one. Instead, defined contribution schemes are the offer, with employees transferring pension risk from one company to another as they progress through their working life. This has the overall effect of people not having the same attachment to an organisation, and so the once-valued job for life no longer exists. Many would argue this is a good thing, but for managers this fragile psychological contract is not easy to balance, which in itself can be a source of workplace stress. But does this paradigm shift alter the view of public servants? In terms of angst, it appears many still cling on to this view of public sector life with almost helpless abandon. Yet we know that employees will be less willing to offer to retire due to financial insecurity that previous pension arrangements (mainly in the public sector) largely negated. We note that this transactional landscape is changing radically; however, the message may be falling on deaf ears?

The second way of looking at working life is through the vocational lens. Occupations such as nursing, policing and fire fighting have often been the preserve of the public-spirited Samaritan with a lifetime of public good at heart. However, it seems increasingly unlikely, for some of the pension reasons mentioned above, that these roles will be seen as 'jobs for life' in the future vision for public services. This could be due to the uncertain nature of public sector work, the financial offering and technological impact or simply because they are seen as unattractive to the new-age entrants to the job market. In Germany, Austria and Switzerland modern apprenticeships are seen as on a par with university education, which seems to offer a modern day approach through which to view a vocation. Although not a new concept, apprenticeships are now used outside what was once the preserve of manually skilled professions, for example in engineering. The UK government has indicated it would consider apprenticeship schemes in future state-awarded contracts and has committed to support three million apprenticeships by 2020. We also see an increase in accredited schemes, such as the Chartered Management Institute degree apprenticeship scheme that projects it will have over 10,000 schemes in train by 2020, and universities being offered attractive (UK) government funding to promote and deliver such schemes. In terms of wellbeing, apprenticeships, in educational terms, have now begun to include habits of the mind, along with the craftsmanship elements of the trade or profession. These habits, grounded in positive psychology, include elements of self-belief, self-control, perseverance, resilience, curiosity, empathy and creativity, and of course craftsmanship. These habits of the mind are all known to impact positively on wellbeing and are a welcome addition to the apprenticeship offering. Such new entry points into working life are significant and should be on the radar of all who have an interest in this book.

A further consideration, and one of the blurred boundaries of the vocational approach to working life, is the seamless merging of private sector contracts into public services. But as we have described, these are not always straightforward and can be confusing to the employees that potentially serve two masters with very different working assumptions. We would suggest here that confusion is not good for one's wellbeing! The current trend of non-financial objectives amongst private sector organisations, predicated on positive social impact, has gone some way to make the workplace even more mysterious to the majority trying to earn a crust.

The third classification of work is what we may view as a *calling*. Although one might be drawn to a religious interpretation, we may view charitable work or volunteer work through this lens too. What drives a person to view work in this way has a very strong connection with meaning and purpose, which are in turn both very closely associated with workplace wellbeing. If work is viewed as a calling, there is very high engagement and a psychological contract, and the recipient can expect maximum discretionary effort to be given. These attributes are very appealing, and for the first time we can see how having effective workplace wellbeing can deliver peak performance from a satisfied and loyal workforce. It is easy to see how the stars can align here: well-organised work, good training, a well-educated workforce that view work as a calling and a worthwhile cause all conspire to deliver the perfect setting. Is it really that simple? As Nita Clarke often says, 'it's the people stupid!', with reference to the seminal 'Engage for Success' work in the UK (MacLeod and Clarke, 2009).

Managing an ageing workforce

The first person to live to be 150 years old has already been born. Reaching 50 years of age traditionally signalled the later years of employ, but now this may not even signal the halfway point of working life. The Government Office for Science (UK) predicts that 12.5 million people will retire from work between 2012 and 2022, and there will be only seven million available to fill those posts, based on birth rate data, and an additional two million jobs being created (Government Office for Science, 2016). Successful management of the future could well be primarily assessed on one's ability to manage constant change, a different workforce demographic, downsizing and fiscal pressure. With governments all across the globe mounting increasingly ferocious programmes of reform, it is not difficult to imagine a state of constant 'unfreeze'. Not quite what Lewin may have had in mind, but managing this will be no easy task. We would hope this book will provide valuable practitioner insight into what works (and what doesn't) and how to 'operationalise' wellbeing in the workplace.

To try to give some sort of indication about what to expect, we have drawn on some interesting data from UK studies. In the light of there being nothing to the contrary being reported in terms of population rates, we assume there is a similar picture globally. In the UK the Chartered Institute of Personnel and Development (CIPD) recently carried out an online survey that asked members what the likely retirement age would be in 2040, with answers ranging up to 74 years old. This presents whole new challenges for managers, in which case it is vital they are equipped with the correct skills to guide them through. The 2014 study carried out by the CIPD projected the age structure of the UK population and calculated the working populous, taking account of the pay as you go state pensions (UK) and the various age classifications, as illustrated in Figure 1.1 below.

The challenge of managing what appears will be an older workforce is still relatively unexplored and likely to throw up many new considerations, with the inevitable reducing talent pool of young people, for example, and an awareness of physical capability. This could be especially pertinent to more labour (physically) intensive public sector work, where clearly the task may simply be too much and

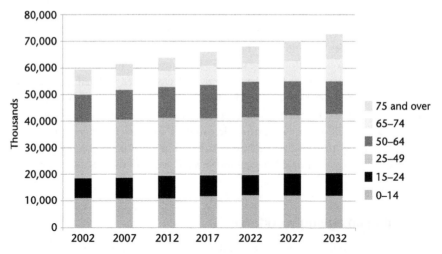

FIGURE 1.1 Age structure of the UK population, 2002–2032 (CIPD, 2014)

Source: ONS 2012 Principal population projections and revised mid-year estimates for 2002 and 2007.

thus adjustments may have to be made to protect the workforce from harm. Managers will have to understand the age characteristics of the labour market, and where once they would be looking to exclude older people, they may now be looking at how to manage the skills and talent pool, and succession planning inclusive of older generations. We see a point not too far into the future where it may be feasible, and probable, to have three generations all at work, top and tailed by a fourth and fifth even that require caring for (young children and elderly relatives). The so-called sandwich generation may be better described as a club (sandwich)! In a 2017 report the CIPD advised employers to keep older workers in the workplace for much longer, calling for an extra one million over 50s to be in work by 2022 to address what they considered to be a widening skills gap in the UK (CIPD, 2017). This will require a host of previously unchartered management skills, education, training and changes in attitudes, parlance and expectations. In the workplace the term 'Granddad' was often reserved for senior employees who were set in their ways. In future one may simply be addressing a related work colleague! In fact, McDonald's, the fast food chain, employs people on attitude, adopting a 'hire the smile' approach. As such, McDonald's claims to have multi-generations in the same workplace on any given shift, and less of a recruitment requirement for qualifications or experience. Research with Lancaster University in the UK reported the best-performing McDonald's restaurants are ones where the mean age is higher: 'mature employees are a key part of the performance recipe', reported Professor Sparrow. The study reported that restaurants employing at least one person over the age of 60 had customer-satisfaction levels 20% higher than those where no one over 50 was employed (Hilary, 2012).

We propose that some of the issues facing members of the older working generation and their employers are recruiting, retraining and indeed retaining. Although these three areas are the focus of many HR departments, both in public and in private, the addition of age poses some challenges. Dealing with recruitment as the first step, the Age in the Workplace report (Age in the Workplace, 2016) estimates that as many as one million people aged 50–64 want to return to the UK workplace. For employees, using age neutral language and avoiding unconscious bias in the selection process can be difficult. Adding to this issues around retraining an elderly workforce and all the potential complications this might involve may put employers off. As we have mentioned, home working, flexible working and remote working are further complications and one may be drawn to the conclusion 'why bother?' However, older workers have years of experience that can add immeasurable benefits to an organisation. In the film *The Intern* a 70-year-old widower played by Robert De Niro applies to be the senior intern in a modern mail order clothing firm and gradually finds his place as a major source of experience and level-headedness within the firm, offering skills and capabilities that many of his younger counterparts cannot. Although an entertaining film, the scenario is such that it cannot be ignored and really highlights the benefits older employees can bring. In a European study, garnering research evidence from the Czech Republic, Denmark, France, Germany and the UK, the Institute for European Studies (IES) noted that employers could not rely solely on a young labour market in a slowly ageing and growing Europe. Employers need to look at the older worker's requirements and make their organisations attractive. A major consideration within this attraction is the notion of supporting the wellbeing of the employee, including welfare support, pension arrangements and end of working life tailing off periods or transition arrangements. The report notes the practice in Denmark of 'Better Working Life for Older Workers', which provides guidance on attaining and retaining the services of older workers, in that case the over 55s (Barslund, 2015). Similar schemes are seen in France, where there have been restrictions on early retirement in the public sector. Germany champions the 'Initiative 50 plus', again seeking to increase the pension age. The UK has a number of schemes, incentives and frameworks, such as the 'Fuller Working Lives' initiative. An observation would be that all of these schemes seem to have a deep concern with retirement benefits, mixed it appears with a recognition of the benefits of the older workforce. Ironically, we often see early redundancy offers being made in the public sector to meet spending review or budgetary reductions. These early retirees then draw on the state in a full circle own goal. Just to finish off the 'it couldn't get any worse scenario', employers then find themselves with huge skills shortages or significant knowledge gaps, often resulting in expensive consultancy to bridge the chasm. One of the big concerns this throws up is the impact all this has on individual wellbeing, and the way they then view work thereafter. This is where the full management skill set is required, to identify where and how 'older' workers can be critical in the organisational setting. As in the *Intern*, this is, on occasion, not immediately recognisable by the unskilled eye.

Technology

We will return to it in greater detail later, but technology is moving at such a pace that it is difficult to even imagine where it may be by 2020 and beyond. Staying with a movie theme, just last year we saw the famous *Back to the Future* vision become largely a reality, aside from the hover-boards of course, although we have very nearly got even there! We now live in an age where mobile phones can help us plan our day and find directions when in an unfamiliar town, or even country. We have technology that can instantly translate languages, recognise songs, our voice commands, turn our heating at home on and off and seemingly endless other applications. But at present these devices are oblivious to how we feel, if our mood is low or high. Maybe these will have developed by 2020? Emotion-aware devices that can detect and interpret human emotions and adapt the lifestyle applications to match, lift or notify us? How will managers use such technology in the workplace? Is this coded life healthy for us? The mind boggles!

It is without doubt that technology has made life so much easier for so many, and even the most sceptical would accept that, in terms of medicine, health and general wellbeing, technology has delivered some pretty swish gadgets to help us out. It has also assisted with safety and monitoring, fire alarms, carbon dioxide levels and so on. It is interesting that about 93% of a flight is controlled by the autopilot, and aviation experts suggest the remaining 7% is pilots merely keeping their hand in. However, there are also what have been termed disruptive technologies, where employees have struggled to cope with the level of ICT knowledge expected of them, so called techno stress. We will look at this in further detail later in the book.

2

WHY WELLBEING, WHY NOW?

Introduction

This chapter will take a look at the journey that wellbeing has been on over recent years, and the regard with which it is held by business in the modern era. Picking up where the previous chapter left off, we move into the 'why?' question. Both literature and practice will be examined, bringing together the argument that successful wellbeing approaches satisfy business leaders that rule with their head and those that rule with their heart. The benefits wellbeing brings to the quality of working life are commonly considered immeasurable, but this chapter will effectively review what is known to date, to quantify how effective wellbeing strategies can benefit fiscal policy as well as emotional transactions, and the *psychological contract*. What are the long-term health benefits associated with this, from both the perspective of the employer and the employee? We ask if the business case for wellbeing is fully made out, using examples from the private sector to inform the argument, where the boundaries are clear; in terms of the bottom line, it is a profitable approach. A UK labour market survey in 2014 reported that 131 million days were lost to sickness absence, that is five days per employee. A recent Health and Safety Executive (HSE, 2017) report put the cost of UK work-related sickness absence in 2014/15 at a staggering £9.3bn, and that was discounting long latency illness such as cancer. However, we would urge caution when viewing workforce wellbeing through the lens of absence management and suggest this is just a small element, and although it is often the issue that grasps the attention of the executive, it is the long-term psychological damage that can be the most significant.

Not just the absence of ill health

It may be prudent at this point to unpack wellbeing a little before we move on. The term, on occasion, is used as a coverall. More and more uses appear every day, and over the years it has moved from a philosophical enquiry into having a more scientific focus. In respect of this book, we attribute it to human life. We major on psychological wellbeing, which has two main aspects: *Hedonic* – feeling good – and *Eudaimonic* – having meaning and purpose. Psychological wellbeing is commonly split into these two areas of study and often will have an evaluative aspect added. Broadly speaking, Hedonic refers to a person's feelings or emotions, whilst Eudaimonic aspects are used to describe the psychological need to live one's life with meaning and purpose. These phrases have been subject to much debate within the wellbeing field. Waterman (1984) claimed:

> The daimon specifies the end or goal (telos) of behaviour. It is the final cause, that, for the sake of which a person acts. It provides purpose and meaning to living. The telic value of eudaimonic feelings rests in the ability to sustain directed action despite the obstacles and setbacks inevitably encountered in the pursuit of those goals deemed to be personally expressive.
>
> *Waterman, 1984, p.16*

According to Ryan and Deci (2001) it is effectively the extent to which a person is fully functioning. Robertson and Cooper observe it as 'the purposeful aspect of psychological well-being' (2011, p.6). Ryff and Keyes (1995, p.720) generated a multidimensional model of wellbeing that included six distinct components of positive psychological functioning:

> In combination, these dimensions encompass a breadth of wellness that includes positive evaluation of one's past life (Self-Acceptance), a sense of continued growth and development as a person (Personal Growth), the belief that one's life is purposeful and meaningful (Purpose in Life), the possession of quality relations with others (Positive Relations With Others), the capacity to manage effectively one's life and surrounding world (Environmental Mastery), and a sense of self-determination (Autonomy).

These six dimensions are referred to as the Eudaimonic aspects of psychological wellbeing. Ryff also opened up debate around wellbeing and age profiles, arguing that there is a definitive relationship between the two. On length of employment, experience and maintaining good psychological health Carol Ryff has written many papers, some of which are fascinating and utilise some well-known academic research, such as that of Carl Jung (personality types) or Abraham Maslow (hierarchy of needs). This work was aptly called 'Happiness is everything, or is it? Explorations on the meaning of psychological well-being'. In it she noted: 'It appears that even well educated, healthy, economically comfortable older adults face significant challenges in their efforts to maintain a sense of purpose and self-realization in later life.' (Ryff, 1989, p.1079). Nearly 30 years on that still holds today!

We acknowledge that wellbeing is dynamic and changes over time, on occasion from minute to minute. John Timpson, the chairman of Timpson, a UK shoe repair company, stated the importance of psychological wellbeing in the workplace: 'being a good listener, who can help anyone hitting a wall of anxiety and depression, is more important than a campaign to cut calories' (Timpson, 2016, p.12). Some types of work can have very high levels of emotional labour, for example policing or end of life care. In these cases the Hedonic elements can almost be removed on occasion; however, there remain high levels of Eudaimonic wellbeing, which really enable employees to continue with these much needed, and more usually public sector, areas of work. The dictionary definition of being comfortable, healthy or happy is only really a starting point, and we would suggest that there is far more to it than this in relation to workplace wellbeing.

The factors illustrated in Figure 2.1 below all impact on our wellbeing in many different ways. Over the course of this book all of these factors will be discussed and we will share our views on each of them with you. The three aspects at the top, Leadership, Resilience and Environment, form the basis of our wellbeing recipe, illustrated in Figure 3.1 later in the book. In a clockwise direction, we look at stress

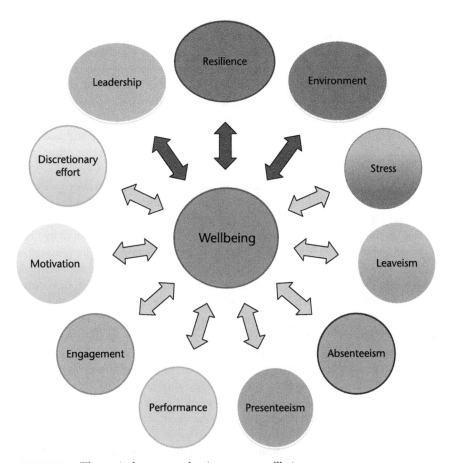

FIGURE 2.1 Theoretical concepts that impact on wellbeing

in some detail in Chapter 4. The concept of leaveism, which we ourselves identified, researched and labelled, is also discussed further in Chapter 4. This provides a fascinating insight into just how wellbeing, or a lack of it, can play out in a practical sense in the workplace. We compare this to descriptions and behaviours associated with presenteeism and the major indicating metric of sickness, absenteeism. As we illustrate though, all three of these must be taken into consideration when we look at employees' wellbeing and their relationship with the workplace. The three subjects that follow will provide clarity on how practitioners can go about this. For those entering either study or the workplace, or for those wanting to know a little more about the subject, this will help you to understand the benefits of getting wellbeing right, in terms of both productivity and performance. If done correctly, this is delivered by members of a workforce that are engaged, motivated and give freely of themselves. Public services are rarely production line activities and therefore rely heavily on discretionary effort, or extra-role effort as it may be known in the US. This phenomenon is at the crux of getting wellbeing right and can provide managers with a useful gauge of how the organisation is doing in terms of the many elements we have discussed already. Almost across the board, you may be able to assume that workers who are fully engaged and motivated will provide high levels of discretionary effort within their work, and we include public service motivation among those motivating factors. Linking engagement to discretionary effort, Towers Perrin (2003) noted that 'another way to think about engagement is the extent to which employees put discretionary effort into their work, in the form of extra time, brainpower and energy' (p.2). This particular report concludes that discretionary effort is the endgame for effective engagement, and acknowledges that 'having a critical mass of employees who freely give that effort is of tremendous value'.

As in all good debate though, there is an opposing view for us to largely dismiss. Taylor, associated with the theory of scientific management (Taylorism), viewed discretion largely in a negative light, arguing that if workers were relied upon to employ high levels of discretion, they would slow down productivity. His approach, which championed rigid supervisory regimes, suggested the removal of as much discretion as possible from the work. At the time (the turn of the twentieth century) jobs with high levels of discretion were only associated with those who worked for themselves, such as farmers or highly skilled craftsmen. The wisdom of the day dictated that work ought to be oriented towards removing as much discretion as possible from the workplace, in an attempt to 'manage out' errors and maximise productivity (Yankelovich and Immerwahr, 1984). As we suggest though, fast forward 100 years or so and the focus is now on unlocking discretionary effort, largely through psychological constructs such as identity, commitment, control and motivation. However, there is a small procedural caution: 'although improved performance and productivity is at the heart of engagement, it cannot be achieved by a mechanistic approach which tries to extract discretionary effort by manipulating employees' commitment and emotions' (MacLeod and Clarke, 2009, p.9).

Financial benefits

Private sector organisations have been quick to pick up on wellbeing in terms of productivity and have gone some way to establishing what this may look like in terms of profitability. Steven Luttrell, the medical director of BUPA, noted that every £1 invested in wellbeing yields a £3 return. These hard-edged fiscal illustrations are not ideal when trying to communicate the right thing to do, but they are helpful for some executives whose sole focus is to drive profit at all costs; and if this is just another tool in the box, then at least they are aware. These individuals will eventually be weeded out as new workforce generations, who have grown up with analytics and are largely unimpressed by the 'toys' available, come through to take the helm.

Wellbeing generally is an important and productive stream of research for all public sector managers and HR professionals because of the significance of stress within the workplace. To give an illustration, stress, the 'health epidemic of the 21st century' according to the World Health Organization, costs American businesses alone an estimated $300 billion a year and is a major threat to the health and wellbeing of people at work (Bruce, 2013). Every year 140 million days are lost to sickness in the UK. UK employers pay £9 billion a year and the state spends £13 billion annually on health-related benefits (Black and Frost, 2011). Over the last five years work-related stress, depression or anxiety has been for each year the single most reported complaint in the UK (HSE, 2008). The Chartered Institute of Personnel and Development (CIPD) absence management survey (CIPD, 2015), involving 592 organisations across the UK (employing almost two million people), reported that average employee absence is 6.6 days per year (falling from 7.7 in 2013). However, UK public sector workers recorded an average of 7.9 days per employee per year (2013: 8.7days, 2012: 7.9 days), and 60% of public sector organisations reported stress-related absence had increased over the last year. If a greater understanding of the relationship between resilience and stress can be achieved, managers and HR professionals will be better able to implement effective support and training interventions, such as resilience training, to assist employees to cope more effectively with the stress that is inherent in today's workplaces.

Psychological benefits

The psychological benefits of wellbeing should be clear, but time and time again we have found ourselves pursuing a two-pronged attack in relation to workplace wellbeing. On the one hand, it seems fairly obvious to us that a workplace where people want to work and where they enjoy work, and where the work is both meaningful and purposeful, should lead to committed, fulfilled employees. These employees work because it gives them a sense of pride and personal satisfaction (in relation to public service as much as anything), the work is well organised and the organisation is well led. The pay is fair, as are the policies and protocols and general social accountability approach to public service undertaken by the organisation. However, for some this is simply not enough and we find ourselves leaning on the financial aspects detailed in the previous section. So we point out fiscal losses, or prevention of fiscal gain, as a rationale for wellbeing. Although this is quite compelling, and often the area the public servant understands best, we long for a time when the majority will see the psychological benefits ranked far above any fiscal position. We would even argue that entrants are beginning to make these a major consideration when entering new employ, rating these above pay and bonus structures and being more focused on considerations such as corporate social responsibility. As part of this responsibility, we would also include an inward facing element: doing the right thing for your own staff. We will discuss later the Workplace Wellbeing Charter in the UK, the successor to the Public Health Responsibility Deal. This framework provides a series of considerations for the psychological benefit of the workforce that if enacted can make the workplace simply a better place. We would argue that, in terms of productivity, attitudes and perceptions, this is clearly a beneficial approach to modern public service delivery. And if the employees are fulfilled, the service delivery will be enhanced.

Creating a business case

This book should, if anything, arm you with sufficient information, theory and evidence to form a business case for your own organisation, or to be in a position to question the existing approach. We have already explained that the business case may have two prongs, which we called the head and heart argument. Balancing these two can be quite challenging, but they are not polar opposites. It very much depends on how you think, what you think is important, how you rank priorities. Whatever is in the mind, the simple fact is that having a considered approach to wellbeing is good for your people, and good for the organisation. We would also challenge the notion that success has to be gained through 'the struggle' and that it is the bedmate of stress. We would suggest that this kind of thinking, especially in senior managers, could be extremely damaging. We acknowledge that on occasion unexpected things happen, stressors can occur, but we would argue this should not be the status quo for organisations; it should be the exception.

So, how to create a business case? We would suggest you start with agreeing what is fundamental to your organisation. What is it all about? Since this book is largely aimed at the public sector, we could probably accept the ultimate 'customer' is the general public of whatever area you work for. That may be national, regional or local. Also, we accept that, although it is a terrible term, some will be 'back office' functions and that the 'customer' may be other parts of the business. Whatever the make-up, we are concerned with people and public service delivery, in whatever guise. It is sometimes useful to view things through the eyes of the private 'money-making' lens to get an idea of criticality. Here we would make the case that if your people are not fit, well and engaged, the business might not be performing as well as it could be, or operating to its full potential. Taking this notion forward, how do we know when our people are not functioning to their full potential? One of the obvious metrics is that of sickness absence figures, and this seems a reasonable place to start. However, we have amassed a decent amount of experience over the years that tells us that when executives start to look at such data, it kick-starts gaming. Here we may see such organisational responses as recovery or recuperative duties, return to work schemes and numerous other weird and wonderful ways of removing an employee from the sickness absence figures, masking the true extent of the issue. Place over this phenomena such as presenteeism and what we uncovered and labelled as leaveism, and you can see how caution is needed when depending on this alone.

Surveying the workforce is an effective way of understanding the problems, and the needs, of the workforce. We have written elsewhere in this book about the use of questionnaires such as ASSET (a short stress evaluation tool), which are self-reporting question sets. Having these professionally analysed and planning a strategic response can be an effective way of addressing employee wellbeing and looking at the causes of stress in the workplace, some of which may not have been immediately obvious in the first instance. It can also be helpful to look at other public service employee strategies, such as leadership, ethics and integrity. We have used these to model how others perceive leadership, and what it may be like to be led by particular employees. All of these can form a suite of management options that can be helpful for governance frameworks, for example. In terms of ASSET, a business case can include elements from these surveys such as having a balanced workload, working relationships, job security, how we deal with change, engagement elements and so on. Viewed through this lens, one can see the benefits that a wellbeing approach can bring. As previously mentioned, and as illustrated in this book, if this does not light the fire, one can always turn to the fiscal consequences of not getting things right. The cost of people over a business lifetime trumps all other costs, especially for public services. In the UK police, for example, 80% of all costs are in people.

Wellbeing and culture

No good book would be worth its salt without a few paragraphs on the subject of the book, i.e. wellbeing, and the interaction with organisational culture, and we figure this should be no different. Bringing wellbeing into public service workplaces is not a new idea, although it is a relatively new practice. This has meant that, for some, a change of approach is required. Some very knowledgeable people have written a great deal about culture, and it is almost inescapable in modern day management literature. The areas that can have the greatest impact on employee wellbeing are how demands are managed, what amount of control people feel they have, having healthy working relationships, the effective management of change, role identity and clarity, and good social support.

There are numerous studies that have examined the influence of a number of aspects of working life, and the existent environmental factors. These studies link learning in an organisation with leadership approaches and the prevailing culture within the organisation. In terms of the bottom line, and as discussed earlier this is the focus for many, the studies found that the culture impacts on the bottom line, or performance as it is often termed. Many suggest culture almost predicts performance, and you can see why this may be so as you start to view how culture impacts in all areas. Now in its fifth edition, Edgar Schein's seminal book *Organizational Culture and Leadership* details many current case studies into leading, learning, culture and of course wellbeing.

One of the seminal pieces of cultural mapping, the cultural web (Johnson et al., 2008), analyses the signs, symbols, routines, structures, power and so on to create an organisational paradigm, 'the way things are done around here'. These frameworks are great ways to assess and snapshot your own paradigms. They can be used as part of a smarter working strategy and also help with formulating an organisational engagement strategy. We will look further at frameworks to garner organisational information in order to inform practice later in the book, and will finish this section with a more in-depth look at the cultural web.

The studies referred to earlier also conclude that a culture that sees innovation and creativity in a positive light, and not all do, is far more likely to enjoy enhanced organisational performance. A further interesting facet is that organisations that have the ability to both learn and unlearn are also more likely to perform better. The unlearning is an important aspect, especially as, as discussed earlier, business is in a constant state of flux. New technologies, ways of working and techniques to manage all replace what some may describe as traditional management practice. So, we could assume that it is better to replace than constantly layer one practice on top of another. This has the additional consequence of confusing new entrants, with old and new ways mixed in an impregnable stew of approaches.

In terms of wellbeing, we have already discussed that we consider the biggest impact on wellbeing to be the role of the first line manager, and creating the cultural environment in which this critical relationship can prosper. So where would you start?

Looking at aspects of work through a cultural lens is in some ways very straightforward. How would a person not connected with the business at all look at this? One of the distinct advantages about public sector work is that you can also ask the question, 'Does this seem like value for money?' In other words, is this something that, if given a choice, people would pay for? We acknowledge that on occasion there are things that public services provide that people simply do not value and yet are an essential part of the bigger picture. Given that, do we make it explicit to our publics that this is the case, and the reasons why? Are we culturally an open organisation? If so, why so, and if not, why not? Asking some of these questions may help you decipher some of the difficult conundrums public service providers are faced with. So what has this got to do with wellbeing?

Well, most people who are attracted to public service work, so research tells us, are giving of themselves. This inner psychology is a powerful tool, and we could argue that a large amount of public service work is delivered through discretionary effort. This is the work we do not necessarily have to do, but which we give up freely due to our inner quest to serve the public. Whether this is true of all public service employees, however, is questionable, and the situation may grow more vague with elements of outsourcing or contracted work beyond the core staff. However, we suggest that this psychological contract is built on a foundation of organisational fairness, in that employees are prepared to work hard, with ethics, honesty and integrity, so long as they feel valued, supported and are treated fairly.

This last point about fairness is probably the crux of this argument. Culturally, fairness is a very big deal. The saying goes that employees join organisations but leave bosses. This is often because they feel they have been treated unfairly. Note that in this respect we say 'feel'. This may be because we are suggesting that these feelings may be in the form of attitudes and perceptions, and not necessarily reality. What an employee may be experiencing is total, across the board, fairness from both the line manager and the organisation. However, if it does not feel that way to the employee, problems can arise, big ones. There has been a whole plethora of literature written about procedural justice and organisational fairness, offering up a varying degree of attribution to different aspects of working life. One thing is for sure though, it should not be overlooked. We also know that a great deal of this does not mirror reality and is purely in the mind of the beholder.

So, having a culture that accepts this, and having people that are culturally aware and self-aware of how their actions, behaviours and words are received by others, are of key importance. If this is not the case within your own organisation, then this is an area that can help you realise huge gains in the exchange of trust.

Some would argue that culture lies beneath the surface of organisations, depicted largely by 'iceberg' models and such. The argument contends that the outgoing façade of the organisation may not represent entirely the inside mechanisms and feel of the workplace. This may be true of many places of work, although this does not indemnify it from critique. Organisations that have managed to achieve success in this respect have realised performance gains in terms of employee wellbeing, productivity and being a great place to work. Indeed, this last aspect has become a very popular way of gauging business success, with more organisations seeking ways to become 'preferred employers' and 'centres of excellence' and so on. The prestige associated with achieving such status has been generally predicated on being seen as a great place to work in terms of employee wellbeing. So there you have it, folks! We will touch on this a little later, but one of the first signs we often see that people are disgruntled is those mutterings of 'intention to leave'.

When employees feel that they are not getting true satisfaction from their work, this very often manifests through withdrawals of discretionary (or free) effort. For those organisations that are forward thinking and conduct regular staff surveys, such feelings are often communicated through question sets looking at intentions to leave or recommend the workplace to others. The answers strongly associated with intention to leave are particularly worrying, and indicative that the wider wellbeing needs of the workforce are not being met. Although some managers may argue that the intention rarely converts to action, it is no less impactive in the workplace. Actually there is an argument that, pragmatically, it is a worse scenario? If people were generally unhappy, disengaged and so on and they did leave, then they could be replaced by a person who wanted to be there, theoretically at least. However, such churn rates are rarely good for the workforce overall, and signs of intention to leave should be given some considerable attention as they are usually indicative of deeper-rooted problems.

One should be mindful that most surveys ask the respondents for subjective opinion and try to elicit attitudes and perceptions of their working life. These are not quite the same as objective reality, but nonetheless they give early indications that, if left unchecked, can translate into organisational problems.

It seems, generally speaking at least, that public services are far less efficient at dealing with this than their colleagues in the private sector. This may be due to more robust performance practices in the private sector and a general production line approach to work not really found in the steadier paced public sector livelihoods? We are, of course, generalising here, but this seems one of the areas in which the two differ?

So how can you gauge culture in the workplace? One way is to use information from the cultural web discussed briefly above. These points, all of equal importance, can help you paint a picture of the culture that exists within an organisation. Of course it is then up to you to decide if this is the culture you wish to have, or indeed thought you had. If not, it can provide you with a place to start to look at why this may be so.

The language used to describe this process has to be carefully considered. It may well be that this type of exercise can be seen as an *audit*, and be compared to other work of a similar nature; or if running it for the first time, it may be useful to refer to it as *analysis*. As discussed later, this type of cultural mapping exercise is designed so that it can be replicated.

When using this sort of approach, it is important to describe how you are defining organisational culture within this context. This is because you are applying an established business descriptor in that it is *the taken for granted assumptions and beliefs that are shared (or a pattern of shared basic assumptions learned, according to Schein, 2010) by people within the organisation, the way people in the organisation think, feel and act; the way things are done at the organisation* (adapted from Deal and Kennedy, 1982).

The importance of this rests in the fact that it is commonly accepted that organisational culture is a key enabler to, and directly influences the strategy of, an organisation. It is viewed as a facilitator for strategic success: 'Cultural constraints determine which strategies are feasible for an organisation and which are not' (Hofstede, 1997, p.373).

It is important for all involved in wellbeing to understand the critical nature that organisational culture plays in successful wellbeing programmes. Large-scale change programmes have been reported through several studies around the world on this very point, Pettigrew in England, Feldman and Barney in the US, and Firsirtou and Rieger in Canada (Mintzberg, 2008). Strategic change may often be reliant on a change in culture, which for practitioners can be very difficult. It is therefore imperative that managers have an understanding of what is going on.

The *cultural web* (Johnson et al., 2008) is a framework for modelling the culture in an organisation. At the centre is the *organisational paradigm*, the collective taken for granted assumptions that people within the organisation have. This is used to diagnose the barriers that may exist to strategic change, and assists with *strategic choices*. It may also be used to inform *change readiness* and *capability assessments* (Balogun and Hope-Hailey, 2008) that are critical to successful wellbeing programmes.

Out of the six aspects, three relate to what are termed soft aspects: *routines and rituals*, *stories* and *symbols*. The other three are unsurprisingly labelled hard aspects: *power structures*, *organisational structures* and *control systems*.

These can be broken down further into three areas that may help in forming a narrative:

1. structures – using information from the cultural web areas of *organisational structures* and *control systems* (hard aspects);
2. political – using the areas of *formal* and *informal power structures*;
3. cultural – using *stories, symbols, rituals and routines* (soft aspects).

To help understand how these can be broken down, you can ask the following questions relating to the organisation. In relation to symbolic elements these could be about badges, crests, how grade or position in the organisation is represented, if at all? In uniformed public services these are usually very apparent, though sometimes not obvious to those outside the particular service. Another area to explore in relation to symbols is the jargon or language used to explain them, how you address leaders, levels of respect, formalities and so on. An interesting aspect of this is to establish if these are any different externally than they are internally, and what that tells you about the culture? Also, does the organisation's strategy reflect reality in this respect? These are all very telling, and deference to hierarchy can paint a picture of what it is like to work at that particular place. This has received a lot of attention in literature relating to blame cultures, learning by mistakes, growth mindsets and so on, and therefore plays a key role. Although described as soft aspects, the resultant gains from understanding can be anything but.

Leading on from this, you can examine routines and rituals in your own, or another's, organisation, an often-fascinating insight and one that can yield great understanding of what is considered important. Again, this may often not be what the organisation thinks it is prioritising. Take a look at what routines are stressed or emphasised, the daily routines, who does what and for whom? Look at who makes the coffee, the structure of the working day, the formality, clocking in and out. What behaviours are encouraged, rewarded, dissuaded, and so on? All of these have a big impact on working relationships and overall wellbeing, and if you have an organisation that encourages and remains contemporary, this can give you a significant competitive advantage. It is often useful to track these rituals back, to see how long they have been going on, the 'it's the way it has always been done around here' type mentality. But as Henry Ford once reportedly said: 'If you always do what you've always done, you'll always get what you've always got!' Another very interesting result of routines and rituals is the workplace behaviours they inevitably drive or promote, some of which you would very often never choose to do purposely. Promotion processes are an area that can be very heavily ritualised in the public sector, and very much to their detriment. We will touch on this again a little later, but if you look at your processes through this lens, it may help clarify some of the, often, nonsense that can occur. A further insight may be garnered from looking at what some of the routines and rituals do for the ethics of the organisation; do they complement, or fly in the face of, the core approach? Do the training programmes that the organisation carries out, or outsources, emphasise the desired state, or is there a complete disconnect between course content and organisational reality? This can be often very telling culturally and is usually indicative that an organisation is perhaps not where it needs to be?

The last area of the three soft aspects reveals another fascinating insight and is that of stories. Carrying on from the previous area, you can question what these stories reflect, and whether they cohere with the day-to-day reality of the workplace? It is often here you encounter the ubiquitous 'war stories' told by the older employees. In public services we often hear accounts of the 'good old days' and the perception that 'morale has never been so low'. Feelings about who are seen as the heroes and villains in the workplace are also pertinent, and perhaps the reason why this is so? One area to take particular note of when exploring the role of stories in cultural mapping is to tease out who are seen as the *mavericks* in the workforce, and why, and if this is seen in a positive light or not? This can reveal what behaviours are condoned, promoted, looked on with disdain or actively prohibited, indicative of the rules both informally and formally that exist in an organisation. One of the issues that impacts on stories is if they convert into informal practices, even though there may be many protocols to follow, that are put in place to protect the organisation from malpractice and so on, stories of people overrelying on experience rather than evidence-based practices, ignoring, reframing or manipulating working directives, applying cognitive filters and the like. This can sometimes explain the distance between working practices that can exist in the same environment when you get a polarised workforce. In terms of wellbeing, this can be a big issue and something an exercise like this can help you surface and deal with appropriately.

Now let's move on to the hard aspects, and what can be seen as the mechanistic, structural or even political workplace practices. In many arenas these operate below the surface and are often not visible to those outside the organisation. For this reason they can be more difficult to establish than the softer aspects. The first of them is control systems, the facets of work that are most closely monitored or controlled, prioritised and viewed as important. If the workforce were asked, what would be the immediate response? Probably more telling is if this response coheres with the organisational purpose, especially in public service. A tell-tale sign is when this is some distance from the aims of the public service. When we talk about meaning and purpose in terms of workplace wellbeing, employees very often can see this as a source of stress, when the job they joined does not seem to accord with the job they find themselves doing. Sometimes you can see some very odd responses when pursuing this line of enquiry, for example the way an organisation rewards or punishes, and where the emphasis lies for those charged with leadership or managerial responsibilities. Is the focus on punitive measures or a growth mindset, where mistakes are allowed and learning takes place from them in an open and transparent manner? It can also be interesting to look at whether controls originate out of strategy, direction or organisational vision, or if they are the result of litigation, defensiveness, guardedness and so on. These may indicate that things have gone astray, and are often the subject of critique in public services. Again, as described in Figure 3.1, we posit the strong connection between this sort of working environment and sub-optimal workforce wellbeing. The number of controls in place can also overwhelm the working populace, but too few can make them nervous, so getting the balance right is important. We link cultural cues to wellbeing here around getting that balance right. It does seem we are fragile creatures at times! An aspect often witnessed in organisations relates to historic or traditional control mechanisms that no longer seem relevant or needed, yet still pervade. We have touched on remote working, virtual offices and the like in other areas of the book, but it does appear this has some way to go. An example is the change in strategy at Yahoo in relation to remote working, flexible practices and what constitutes the workplace. It is interesting to look on as some of the early adopters change tack on this and revert back. Looking through the lens of control systems may well give greater insight into why this is so.

Organisational structures are a fascinating topic of their own and have been the subject of much analysis over the years, with books dedicated to that very subject alone. Taking a look at the organisational chart of any company can be quite an experience, and very rarely identifies where all the power lies, or even where it should lie on occasion! Are the hierarchies flat or multi-faceted? Are the structures formal or informal? This is another area where paradox can exist. Many propose flattening the hierarchy, but then again many championed open-office environments as a gold standard! One of the areas that can promote the big 'reveal' is to look at whether or not the structure promotes collaboration or competition, and if this is healthy in either direction? What sort of real power do these structures support, or even seem to support? We can tease out where the real power lies. Sometimes in an organisation bureaucratic roles seem to harvest power, the director's secretariat, the impregnable diary of the CEO, administrative assistants, payroll, transport managers and so on. Although these roles have very little to do with the public service's key business, they can nevertheless make the difference between a straightforward func-tion or one that is wrapped in an envelope of bureaucratic nonsense that often drives the workforce crazy! When surveyed, employees often promote the stress of this over their key role objectives.

This leads us nicely on to the issues around power structures, the last of the hard aspects, and how these are distributed in an organisation. This power structure aspect is probably the largest issue that impacts on wellbeing. How an organisation arranges work, how it sets the tone, what sort of management behaviour or style is encouraged or championed undoubtedly create the largest impact on the individual. People join organisations but leave managers it is oft said. Formal and informal power can also be difficult to understand absolutely. Psychology can be at full throttle here, with numerous phenomena playing out, both good and bad. Take wellbeing, for instance; some will champion this, realising that a workforce that is treated well is far more likely to offer up great performance and ultimately productivity. Others would argue that workers should do as their superiors tell them, and if they do not, sanctions ought to follow. However, the workplace is rarely this simple, and a look at cultural power can help you clarify what is going on. Discipline cultures can seem attractive to some (not us, we hasten to add) and somehow linked to high performance. Indeed, the days of new public management, where 'things' were measured and somehow put forward as units of production, are still evident in many public services. Power and performance are very interesting bedfellows. Very seldom is it obvious how this succeeds, but good organisations always seem to have almost unseen power structures, are open to outside scrutiny and workers talk positively about life within the organisation. Sometimes, though, complex work requires differing approaches to, let's say, a production line. As not many public services involve production line activity, it is better to look at power structures in an objective fashion. Power holders can sometimes dress (to impress) differently from the general working population. Again, in many successful companies where productivity is high you do not see this distinction as overtly. It is interesting to seek out the core assumptions of managers, and how these relate to power. Meetings can give another valuable insight – who attends, who speaks, who is on the agenda, and so on. In terms of wellbeing, we consider managers with high levels of people skills are often good change agents, sensitive to staff, empathetic and, as a direct result, experience high levels of trust, loyalty and productivity from their workforce. All these are known, from our own and others' research, to improve wellbeing.

We include these cultural, structural and political aspects of the wellbeing arena to illustrate how culture plays a huge part in the management of wellbeing and can give valuable insight into organisational environments. We are looking here at what works in the workplace, and why this may be so, and how we learn from these hard and soft aspects and manage them in our own workplaces or those we come into contact with.

3

WELLBEING

The fundamentals

Introduction

Having made a case for wellbeing in the previous chapter, we now move on to suggest a framework for getting started with wellbeing in the workplace, with these three fundamental tenets: personal resilience, creating the right environment and aligning your leaders. In this chapter we will reference quite a bit of academic research, which we hope will provide a further source of reading and an evidence base for our claims. Although some of these studies, like most academic literature, may feature contested views, we consider them to be the best sources of reference at the time of writing and therefore include them for information. All three of our tenets are discussed in depth, with supporting evidence from the field, to provide a framework from which teams, departments, business units and organisations can build an effective wellbeing approach in the workplace. Evidence is exhibited of an approach that is grounded on a successful model that has been proven to work in practice in the UK public service sector. Examples are given of how creating the right environment can impact significantly on the health and wellbeing of the workforce. How the physiological, psychological, sociological and financial aspects of wellbeing all have a part to play will be modelled in this chapter. These things are done through the actions of good/ethical leaders/managers, together with the personal resilience of employees and correct amounts of work–life balance, healthy lifestyles and meaning and purpose in working life.

What we suggest is that you try all this out in whatever work setting you happen to be. Nothing is more convincing than to see theoretical models working in practice, and here is where we posit this book will be of real use to those either studying or practising. Particular relevancy is to be seen in the utilisation of the model above. The first step is to explore the content of this to see if it resonates with the workforce you are interested in. We find this initial enquiry stage is

Environment	Leadership	Resilience	Employee wellbeing
Creating an environment in which all employees can lead a meaningful and purposeful life.	Knowing enough about your staff to be able to recognise when things are not right, and to have the skills to intervene both quickly and effectively.	The ability to cope with adversity, and to be able to 'bounce back'. Being able to deal with the stressors of every day life.	• Psychological • Physiological • Sociological • Financial

FIGURE 3.1 Organisational recipe for wellbeing

Source: Copyright © Hesketh, 2014.

particularly important. It also provides confidence that the content accords with people. Towards the end of this book we hear accounts from leaders in organisations who have actually put it into practice, and hear how effective strategies on wellbeing are in real-life public sector working environments. These accounts give readers an opportunity to test their thoughts against those of others, to see if the themes resonate, and if the working environment can be improved by subtle incremental changes in practice, perhaps coupled with having a growth mindset.

Personal resilience

Personal resilience is broadly viewed as the antidote to stress. The discovery of stress is commonly attributed to Hans Selye, who in 1935 identified the syndrome in laboratory rats (Viner, 1999; Cooper, 2004). He later suggested the notion that there may be good stress, which he termed *eustress*, as opposed to *distress* (Selye, 1984). Since then the theory has been developed, and a contemporary view of stress is often seen as being the point after which the amount of pressure a person is under exceeds their ability to cope, while conceding that some pressure is actually good for you. There may be a different 'set point' for everyone, dependent on skills, capability, personality, etc. 'It has to be recognized that stress is dynamic and, in a rapidly changing environment, is unlikely to ever disappear completely, but needs to be regularly monitored and addressed.' (Cooper and Cartwright, 1997, p.12). As well as traditional descriptions associated with stress through too much work, i.e. overload, employees can experience stress by having too little to do, causing boredom, apathy and frustration, which can be equally stressful (Palmer and Cooper, 2010). Figure 3.2 shows this relationship and is adapted from the seminal work of Yerkes and Dodson.

These dimensions form the basis of resilience programmes that have been developed to equip workers with the necessary tools to recognise and act in respect of their own personal circumstances. It would seem, then, that if stress is ever present, so too should be mechanisms to confront it. Resilience is the prime mechanism,

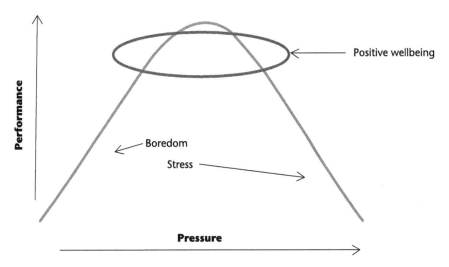

FIGURE 3.2 Performance–pressure relationship

Source: Adapted from Yerkes and Dodson (1908).

and therefore those equipped with the knowledge and skill to be aware of, and improve, their resilience ought to function better in the workplace. Resilience is a combination of personal characteristics and learned skills. These learned skills could include thinking differently, for example using CBT techniques to reframe negative thoughts. They can include having the ability to deal with both success and failure, and developing a positive attribution style. Other learned skills can centre on coping strategies, self-mastery, making the most of personal (signature) strengths and learning to work smarter. All these are proven to increase personal resilience.

In terms of personal resilience, speaking in a UK radio interview, the President of the Royal College of Psychiatrists in the UK, Sir Simon Wessely, noted that actually people are a bit tougher than we generally think (BBC, 2017). Basing his argument on research with Second World War survivors, he proposed that, in relation to research on modern day terrorist attacks, most people do not require any mental help assistance in overcoming traumatic events, and in fact some of the interventions can make the subjects worse off. He argued that interventions such as post-event diffusing sessions were subject to randomised control trials, a robust research methodology used in the majority of scientific research, and seemed to actually have a detrimental effect.

The word 'resilience' itself has roots in the Latin verb *resilire* – to rebound, to return to normal. The various definitions share talk about elasticity, so notions of being stretched and returning to shape could be conjured up. In Figure 3.1 (see p. 34) we have split resilience into two features: coping with adversity and being able to bounce back. We will unpick those a little later, but first we will take a look at the views some academics have given about what resilience is. We have provided some of the more popular interpretations of resilience in a workplace context but concede there are a good deal more out there. However, to cohere with the narrative appended to the model, we draw upon some of the following explanations.

In terms of the public sector, a great deal of research on resilience has focused on the emergency and caring professions such as the police (Paton, 2006), army (Cornum, 2012), ambulance service (Gayton and Lovell, 2012), nursing (Zander et al., 2013), and social work (Grant and Kinman, 2013). We assume that this is probably because of the high levels of stress experienced in these roles, all of which draw heavily on emotional labour. We will link this to *empathy* later in the chapter. For now we will try to highlight some of the global interpretations of resilience that accord with our own model above, and which can be both measured and analysed by survey instruments. This allows us to effectively establish what works in terms of addressing personal resilience, which is discussed in Chapter 4.

In a US study aimed at identifying and treating individuals at risk of post-trauma, Haglund et al. suggest resilience refers to the 'ability to successfully adapt to stressors, maintaining psychological wellbeing in the face of adversity' (2007, p.899). Two of the co-authors of this paper were Southwick and Charney, who developed a 'resilience prescription' founded upon experiences of prisoners of war (Southwick and Charney, 2012b). They were particularly interested in how some people were able to bounce back from adversity and some were unable to do so, which even extended to people who had experienced the same traumatic events.

Ann Masten from the University of Minnesota, writing about global perspectives on resilience in children following natural disasters, suggests it is 'the capacity of a dynamic system to adapt successfully to disturbances that threaten system function, viability, or development' (2014, p.6). Her study drew on reports from the United Nations about post-disaster coping after events such as tsunamis, earthquakes, conflicts and other disasters. She was interested in what makes individuals resilient and who stays well and recovers well, and how, using what is arguably the most extreme of samples to study. She concluded, positively, that resilience is made up of ordinary processes, and a book followed that detailed her work, aptly called *Ordinary Magic: Resilience in Development* (2014).

Larry Mallack, researching resilience amongst healthcare providers in the US and developing a Workplace Resilience Instrument, described resilience as 'the ability of an individual or organization to expeditiously design and implement positive adaptive behaviors matched to the immediate situation, while enduring minimal stress' (1998, p.148).

Fred Luthans, who writes largely about positive organisational behaviour and developing and managing psychological strengths, defines resilience as the 'positive psychological capacity to rebound or bounce back from adversity, uncertainty, conflict, failure or even positive change, progress and increased responsibility' (2002, p.702). Luthans is of a view that optimistic, energetic people who enjoy life can be a major attribute to an organisation, a view we would echo. Luthans' definition highlights the well-known and important 'bouncing back' (or rebounding) aspect of resilience and is useful in drawing attention to the extensive need for resilience in both positive (opportunities or advancement) and negative (dealing with adversity) experiences in the workplace. He makes mention of bouncing back in terms of something that can be learned or enhanced through mastery. Luthans' notion about the ability to 'bounce back' from adversity, or rebound, seems to make perfect sense, although the origins of the phrase 'bouncebackability' appear to be ascribed to the 'great philosopher' Ian Dowie (a UK football pundit) in his descriptions of a woeful season for Crystal Palace (a UK football team)!

Brigadier General Rhonda Cornum (Cornum, 2012) suggests that the things that enable a person to 'bounce back' are not all due to an individual's make-up, and effective coping strategies can be learned and developed. Up until recently Dr Rhonda Cornum, a surgeon, was Director of the US Joint Soldier Fitness Programme. This programme introduced pre-deployment resilience training, amongst other things, for members of the armed forces and subsequently their families. Both Cornum and Casey (of VUCA fame) were heavily involved with the development and implementation of this ground-breaking programme. The careers of both these soldiers make for fascinating reading, Cornum was shot down in a Black Hawk helicopter during the Gulf War and held prisoner, giving her first-hand experience of the ultimate in resilience challenges.

As emotions are critical, research on emotional resilience has linked people's physical and emotional reactions and seeks to explain why the body reacts in the way it does and to offer useful strategies to help overcome the negative reactions and effects. Douglas Paton, who studied trauma in police officers' claims in relation to critical incident stress, such as the well-known condition of PTSD, stated that there can be 'both positive (e.g., posttraumatic growth) and negative outcomes (e.g., learned avoidance of threat situations)' (2006, p.198).

Dr Sam Goldstein, an American neuropsychologist, shifted the approach in his work with children from that of trying to find out what was wrong to studying what methods people could employ to overcome some of the adversity we have discussed. His focus was on how children who have experienced huge levels of adversity then went on to lead successful and happy lives by fostering strength, hope and optimism. His observations were that increasing stress, pressure and demands on schoolchildren (in the US) were leading to health disorders, and a huge rise in depression amongst school-age children. He concluded, in support of what we have already established to a large extent, that resilience held the keys to solving many of these problems. Goldstein also suggested that resilience, which he described as the ability to cope and feel competent, could overcome a genetic predisposition. His argument was that lived experiences, understanding of ourselves and the ability to think positively and overcome day-to-day challenges in life could supersede biological make-up.

One of the areas receiving a burgeoning amount of attention in public services, and to some extent the private sector, is investment in employee resilience training. With entrepreneurs across the globe positing the benefits to organisations, it seems to be a growth industry. But, as we will suggest here, if organisations are going to invest money, time and effort into resilience training, it is better to take the time to establish the needs of both the organisation and the individuals working within it before embarking on the journey. Having published numerous academic papers on the subject, we can say with some authority that such an important decision, in terms of both financial and emotional investment, ought to be made carefully and considerately. If the training, delivered professionally and in the context of the working environment, is to be effective, we suggest it is well worth investing in a professional outfit that has credibility and a reputation for quality. Some of our own research has shown negligible impact when this is not so. However, incredible results, including sustainable performance over time, are achievable when the training is delivered professionally.

One area that has been contested over recent years is whether it is worthwhile for organisations to train up their own people to deliver resilience training, and the pros and cons associated with this practice. In many public services, centralised L&D and HRM departments may find themselves being asked to deliver this sort of service. We suggest that, unless there are professionals in those departments, it is better left to the experts. However, it seems the benefits of refresher training and such may be appropriately delivered in discursive in-house sessions, perhaps in the vein of peer support.

Creating the right environment – engagement

Creating the right environment in the workplace is no easy task, perhaps one of the toughest managers face. It takes a lot of effort and a deep understanding of the concepts at play. The *culture*, the *identity*, the *organisational paradigm* – these are all phrases that can be associated with creating the right environment. The links between *resilience*, *leadership* and the relationship with *discretionary effort*, and the importance of effective *engagement*, are all academically robust and play a key role in getting things right. We use the construct of *engagement* as a central theme to pull these elements together and illustrate how those charged can create, and influence others in creating, a working environment congruent with employee wellbeing. Engagement has become one of the highest priorities for organisations around the globe, but whilst managers are fully aware of the importance of a highly engaged workforce, very few seem to understand what practices drive and sustain high levels of engagement.

In terms of *engagement*, it may be prudent to explain what exactly we are talking about here, what definition we are attributing to it in a working context. People have a choice about how much of themselves they offer up at work, what sort of level of investment they have in the organisation, and the function it performs. Closely associated with discretionary effort, employees must feel that their work has meaning and purpose, that it is worthwhile, and that somehow they contribute to the collective effort. In a study of engagement and burnout in Spanish workers and students at a university, Schaufeli et al. (from Utrecht University in the Netherlands) offered a definition of workplace engagement as 'a positive, fulfilling, work-related state of mind that is characterized by vigor, dedication, and absorption' (2002, p.74). What is particularly interesting, although in a fairly negative light, is that their study noted that the majority of academic study focused on the negative outcomes; they suggested a ratio of 15:1. So they looked at what the positive outcomes were, and how they were brought about, largely through the lens of engagement. So *engagement* can be a way we view interactions positively. Each of their elements of vigor, dedication and absorption have further descriptions that are closely related to Positive Psychology, such as *flow,* described by Martin Seligman (Seligman, 2003), and *subjective wellbeing or happiness* (Diener, 2000). We will discuss the seminal work of Seligman and Diener later in the book.

Robertson and Cooper (2010) proposed that, to maintain high levels of sustainable employee engagement, employee wellbeing should also be high, and this can be achieved through 'full engagement' and not just a commitment-based (organisational) view of the concept. In support, an analysis of sickness in hospital employees in Copenhagen, Denmark, found that those who experienced high levels of meaningfulness in their job and those who had trusting relationships with their immediate supervisors were far less likely to take sickness absence (Suadicani et al., 2014). Interestingly this study also looked at when an employee has an *intention to leave* an organisation and the relationship this has with their sickness absence. We have suggested that *intention to leave* does not automatically result in actually leaving but can result in employees effectively 'playing up' if they are in this state of mind, i.e. disengaged from work and/or the workplace. As alluded to earlier, in terms of sickness absence, research indicates that engaged workers take on average 2.69 and the disengaged take 6.19 days sickness per year (Rayton et al., 2012). We would suggest that this doubling between engaged and disengaged is a great means by which to view the benefits that effective engagement can provide to an organisation. These figures originate from the well-known Engage for Success programme in the UK, which reported that only a third of workers in the UK are engaged. They also suggest that engagement directly impacts on productivity and performance.

There is an acknowledgement that employees can, in fact, be too committed and too engaged with their work. One should also take care not to relate working hard with *burnout*. We suggest burnout, or mental weariness as it has been referred to, occurs when working at 85–100% of one's capacity over long periods of time, i.e. as almost the norm. It has been established that burnout is not the antipode of engagement (Schaufeli and Bakker, 2004). Bakker, in research carried out in four different service organisations in the Netherlands, describes people who are too engaged and too committed as 'workaholics' or 'work addicts' and distinguishes them from employees who experience authentic engagement in their work, who, they argue, have outside interests (societal wellbeing) and find their work enjoyable and fun (Bakker and Demerouti, 2008); this is similar to the concept of being in 'flow', according to Seligman, who describes it as 'being at one with the music, time stopping, and the loss of self-consciousness during an absorbing activity' (2011, p.11). These 'addicts' may materialise through concepts such as *presenteeism*, when an employee attends work whilst they are actually unwell or puts in 'face time' to indicate their dedication to work (Johns, 2010); or *leaveism*, a term we introduced, following research, to describe when an employee takes part of their annual leave entitlement to have time off work when they are actually unwell, or who take work on holiday or home that they cannot complete in their contracted hours (Hesketh and Cooper, 2014). Therefore it is important to delineate, and establish, what behaviour it is that employees are exhibiting: *highly engaged* or *addicted*? These concepts are not easily defined or interpreted and, as with leaveism, we note that our conceptualisation can be viewed through either a positive or a negative lens. For example, it could be argued that employees should not feel the need to take annual leave if they feel unwell. However, for a variety of reasons, employees feel better taking this route. Now, we do not condone some of the reasons offered; for example, the fear of being dismissed or viewed in a bad light is clearly not a good thing. But, if employees feel an overwhelming need to show loyalty and are proud of an unblemished sickness record (albeit not authentic), then this option may actually make them feel better. Who are we to judge? And likewise with taking work home – although clearly a sign of workload overload, some employees may wish to take their time and not feel hurried. It may be their way of reducing internal stress levels, so they may show high self-awareness traits? Again, the reasons are unclear, and probably very subjective dependent on circumstances, so we may reserve judgement until further research has been carried out to establish why this occurs in the workplace. One thing is for sure, and that is that it is prevalent, and it would appear that the higher up in an organisation an employee gets, the more likely it is that it will occur.

A US study concluded that high performance, positive attitudes and lower staff turnover are all cited as positive outcomes of a highly engaged workforce (Crawford et al., 2010), whilst research in the UK police suggested that employees who are masking illness or taking work on holiday may actually be working over their limits of resilience (Hesketh et al., 2015b). In research carried out in Austria, Gerich suggests that high workload seems to predict sickness presence, whereas fear of job loss appears to promote leaveism (2015). Wiley (2009) suggests that as few as a third of workers are engaged in the UK. He claims that the leadership behaviours and practices can be very different in organisations seeking a high engagement workforce, evoking trust and confidence in senior leaders, which he argues leads to high performance as a direct consequence. He concedes this high performance is delivered, to a large extent, via discretionary effort. It appears that once again leadership plays a key role, especially the line management of individuals (their immediate supervision); they are critical to creating the right environment for employees to engage proactively (Hesketh et al., 2014b). These environmental aspects were discussed in great detail in the (UK) government sponsored review of workplace engagement mentioned earlier (MacLeod and Clarke, 2009). Line managers are not only required to know their staff in almost familial ways, but it is incumbent on leaders to ensure work is also challenging. Crawford et al. argue that work demands that are viewed as a *hindrance* by employees are related negatively to engagement, but work demand that is *challenging* (even if difficult) is positively related to engagement (2010, p.835). We could also make similar links to conceptualisations of presenteeism and leaveism, whereby the underlying rationale directs the perceived orientation of the subject. So in many ways both phenomena can be viewed positively or negatively, dependent on the thought processes of the employees themselves. This is similar to the views of discretion and discretionary effort.

We now take a brief look at the working origins of these terms, which ought to clarify why we think like we do, and the thought processes of managers charged with applying the concepts. Linking engagement to discretionary effort, Towers Perrin note that 'another way to think about engagement is the extent to which employees put discretionary effort into their work, in the form of extra time, brainpower and energy'. This particular report concludes that discretionary effort is the endgame for effective engagement, and acknowledges that 'having a critical mass of employees who freely give that effort is of tremendous value' (2003, p.2). Taylor, associated with the theory of scientific management (Taylorism), viewed discretion largely in a negative light, arguing that if workers were relied upon to employ high levels of discretion, they would slow down productivity. His approach, which championed rigid supervisory regimes, suggested the removal of as much discretion as possible from work (at the time largely focused on production line activities in industrial America). In that period (the turn of the twentieth century) jobs with high levels of discretion were only associated with those who worked for themselves, such as farmers or highly skilled craftsmen. The wisdom of the day dictated that work ought to be oriented towards removing as much discretion as possible from the workplace, in an attempt to 'manage out' errors (*Poke Yoke* in Systems Thinking terms) and maximise productivity (Yankelovich and Immerwahr, 1984). Fast forward 100 years or so and the focus is now concerned with unlocking discretionary effort, largely through psychological constructs such as identity, commitment, control and motivation. However, there is caution: 'although improved performance and productivity is at the heart of engagement, it cannot be achieved by a mechanistic approach which tries to extract discretionary effort by manipulating employees' commitment and emotions' (MacLeod and Clarke, 2009, p.9). To conclude, we view discretion and discretionary effort in positive terms, but it is clearly not seen like this by all, and many command-and-control approaches still have Taylorism at their heart.

Creating the right environment for a workforce to experience meaning and purpose in their work is very often easier said than done, with a multitude of challenges and issues to deal with on a daily basis. These may range from supplier problems to customer complaints, but the binding phenomenon will often be how these groups of people feel about the way they have been treated. And we say feel because it may not be reality; the perception is often the thing that judgement is made upon. This can almost be to an extent where actually what is reality is either awful or fantastic. It is the way people feel that is often what is acted upon. This was probably best summed up by poet and civil rights activist Maya Angelou in her beautiful words (quoted in Rathus, 2012, p.246): 'I've learned that people will forget what you said, people will forget what you did, but people will never forget how you made them feel.' She herself was a superb example of personal resilience and we would recommend taking the time to look at her life history. Sadly, she died in 2014.

How people feel, how they perceive work and their approach are critical for wellbeing. Organisations, for all the right reasons, can do all the wrong things. Incentivising work is one such approach that can cause great angst and division in the workplace. It may not be badged as such; in some public sector organisations they call it reward and recognition. We would urge caution when setting up and embedding such schemes in the workplace. The unintended consequences can be quite damaging to staff. Monetary incentives are a good example. It seems that nobody really wants to reveal his or her own earnings, or bonuses. This leads to awkward conversations and feelings of envy or jealousy – and yet we take this and somehow believe that incentivising further will result in productivity. Employees already view salary points with great suspicion. Doing the same job as your co-worker and being paid more or less solely because of the number of years you have been at the firm always seems wrong, even though most public sector employers use this payment model. We do advocate reward by way of good management, for example being told you have done a great job, when deserved of course. This is another pitfall; inauthentic platitudes for the sake of it that nobody really believes can also be damaging. So, the rewards need to be authentic; otherwise the result will be the unintended consequence that workers, for example, may not feel valued, trusted or job secure.

Later in this book we will explore how organisations can gauge this 'feeling' by using effective survey instruments to measure the attitudes and perceptions of the workforce. This is particularly useful when conducting interventions, such as resilience training, to see if they have made any difference to the workforce or not. What is really interesting is the very low impact that features such as pay have on these feelings. Study after study places remuneration very low on the wellbeing scale, and although a component of job satisfaction, once wellbeing metrics are employed it features very low down, if at all. Features such as psychological safety, meaningful work, good leadership, security and good working relationships are high on the concern list for employees.

So what does the physical environment look like, tangibly? Are we talking about things such as Biophilia? Or is it the way things get done, or other cultural artefacts? Or is it a mixture of all these things? Let us spend a little time discussing some of the aspects of a fascinating concept known as Biophilia. It has been described as the 'innate tendency to focus on life and lifelike processes' by Edward Wilson (1984), who wrote an interesting book of the same name on the subject. So how does this relate to the workplace? The modern office space has changed dramatically over the years. The UK TV drama *Mr Selfridge* illustrated this very well, with the individual offices of the administration staff arranged along a dark wood-clad corridor, the innards masked by opaque glass and intricate lead beading. Now we see big open-plan office space. But which is better for the workforce? The open-space offices can be extremely noisy, and we would suggest are better suited to extroverts. Some proponents argue that the open office lends itself to greater collaboration and is better for camaraderie. Some commentators argue that it is less likely to lead to increased wellbeing and productivity and there is no privacy. We have reported previously on how open-plan offices can lead workers to perceive they are being treated as units of production, very much like a piece of office equipment, and as such can feel undervalued and experience low job satisfaction and decreased meaning and purpose. In the office environment, the notion of Biophilia involves the introduction of plant life into the workspace, good air quality in the office and having plenty of windows (natural light) for workers to look out onto natural scenes. Interestingly, views of busy roads seemingly have the opposite effect.

Aligning your leaders

Leadership plays such a huge part in the wellbeing landscape that it cannot be anything other than at the forefront of the minds of those charged with public services. The skills required to lead public services, as alluded to earlier, are very different from what they were just a few years ago. The pace and scale of change facing public service employees are unprecedented, and leaders need to be alert to the dynamic needs of their workforce. We simplified this in our model in Figure 3.1 as the ability to know enough about one's employees to notice when things are not right and to have the skills to intervene quickly and effectively. What we are saying here is that employers, managers, leaders and all those charged with people responsibility should be trained, educated and knowledgeable in dealing with people on an emotional level. Although sometimes referred to as 'soft skills', we would argue that these are amongst the most difficult tasks a modern day supervisor faces, and to be competent requires self-actualisation, sensitivity and attention. We were concerned about the small amount of management training in the public sector that had a focus on wellbeing, and the competency levels of leaders when dealing with wellbeing issues. Fundamentally, we would hope that this book goes some way to helping leaders both understand wellbeing and resilience and create workplace environments where employees can prosper and draw meaning and purpose from their everyday working life. They can feel secure, have a good work–life balance (or integration, as we would suggest), have good working relationships and generally feel they are leading a fulfilling and worthwhile life that contributes to society as a whole.

A simple way to consider effective leadership is by focusing on three aspects, which we have labelled here as 1) knowing your staff, 2) knowing your stuff and 3) knowing yourself. As depicted in Figure 3.3, these are interlinked, and we argue that all three elements are vital for successful workplace leadership outcomes. Taking a simple view of each of these in turn may be fruitful here. Whilst we do not wish to go into a journey of discovery, it is important to know how you yourself both operate and are viewed by those around you. Your own leadership style is something you need to be conscious of. How that style impacts on others is also critical for employee wellbeing. We all have a view of what good looks like, but it is important to keep in mind your overall effect. Knowing yourself can be the hardest part of this offering, but equally one that can yield the largest rewards, for you personally and for those around you. Knowing those around you can pay dividends too

FIGURE 3.3   A simple leadership model: knowing your stuff, staff and self

and can be increasingly challenging in the era of remote or virtual working, home working, flexible working and so on. Having a plan around workforce engagement is important here and can be key to followership. Equipping staff, trusting them, having strong relationships and the right attitude are all issues to consider. Finally we need to be operationally competent, which we have labelled 'knowing your stuff'. Being from the north of England, we thought this added a gritty edge to our model, à la Sean Bean! Sometimes this can be overlooked, in spite of the numerous pieces of research that tell us that the workforce consider it essential that leaders know about the work they are doing, and preferably have done it before themselves. We understand that, especially with the technical advancements being made, this is not always possible, but we would expect leaders to consider how they would feel about being led by somebody with no grasp at all of what their role entailed?

Discretionary effort

The term is used to describe the amount of effort people are prepared to give of themselves voluntarily. Known as extra-role effort in the US, it describes behaviours that cannot be prescribed or perhaps required, or that may run into trouble if pre-scribed, i.e. you will be nice to customers. It includes gestures, manners, niceties, common decency, loyalty (when nobody is looking!) and so on, such as looking after company equipment, being kind to colleagues, going the extra mile and so on. The reason it is so important in terms of leadership is that it is very often the leader or manager that inspires or motivates someone to give more of themselves than they are contracted to do, to be more positive in the workplace, be happier and so on. The immediate supervisor, according to Bateman and Organ (1983), represents the most direct source of variance in the exchange affect of discretionary effort, and thus they play a (if not the) crucial role. We highlight the positive importance also because public services, by their very nature, depend heavily on high levels of discretionary effort. Although we have touched on this in other parts of the book, we will explain the hypothesis behind our thinking here. Having a good understanding of this, in terms of management, will return you an increase in performance, and beyond.

Discretionary effort, we argue, can be as much as 50% of an employee's productivity. We suggest the terms performance and productivity can be interchanged for the benefit of this illustration, dependent on how service is viewed within a particular organisation. As we note, much of the work of public services is not involved in making a product, though there will be exceptions to this of course. What we suggest is that providing a service is not an easy notion to fully understand. What is a service? Who is the customer for each interchange? How do we know if the customers are satisfied with the service they receive? What is apparent is that it is beneficial if public service workers engage fully with their publics. We suggest that, in order to avoid burnout, a sustainable work rate may be 85%, basing this on operations management literature; see, for example, the Coping Zone (Johnston and Clark, 2008). When we now look at the minimum work effort required, that is just enough to stay out of trouble, avoid a sanction and so on, this, we hypothesise, could be as low as 35% (see Figure 3.4). This leaves 50% of what we are going to call, by way of illustrating the point, discretionary effort.

We know most of this effort is driven by the relationship an employee has with their employer, and studies have shown that leadership has a huge role to play in this; see, for example, our study of discretionary effort and engagement in policing (Hesketh et al., 2016). So what can leaders expect from this discretionary effort in terms of workers' productivity? In a longitudinal study in the US this effort consisted of helping co-workers with their work, keeping the workplace clean and tidy and free from physical dangers, enjoying good working relationships, and such (Bateman and Organ, 1983). Wiley (2009) suggests that as few as a third of workers are engaged in the UK. He claims that the leadership behaviours and practices can be very different in organisations seeking a high engagement workforce, evoking trust and confidence in senior leaders, which he argues leads to high performance as a direct consequence. He concedes this high performance is delivered, to a large extent, via discretionary effort. Also making links to engagement, the seminal work in the UK of MacLeod and Clarke (2009) on 'Engage for Success' noted that the focus is now on unlocking discretionary effort, largely through psychological constructs such as identity, commitment, control and motivation. The implication for managers who focus on high engagement, and are cognisant of the concept of discretionary effort, is that they can expect a high return on that focus. Together with employee wellbeing generally, these returns can be substantial in terms of performance and/or productivity, as well as improved working relationships. As a result of employing high levels of discretionary effort, managers will find that their people will be inspired and motivated to carry out their duties with meaning and purpose, resulting in sustainable high levels of quality and performance. We will look at meaning and purpose in ethics shortly, but a further consideration may be that as the nature of the modern workplace evolves, and knowledge workers move to more flexible, remote or virtual practices, the impact that discretionary effort has on the bottom line should not be overlooked or underestimated. Based on research relating to engagement, and linking the two concepts,

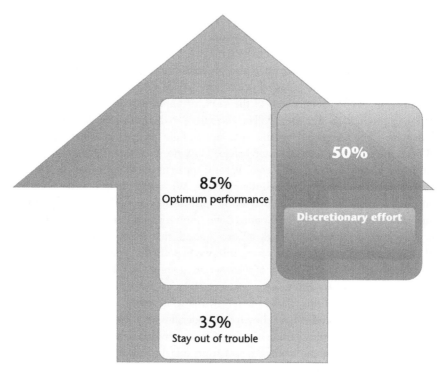

FIGURE 3.4 Hypothesis for discretionary effort

unlocking or realising this will deliver a high and sustainable return. In terms of adding public value, popularised by Hartley, Benington, Alford and Moore, it may also go some way to answering the questions posed earlier in this section.

Ethical leadership

When thinking about ethics and ethical behaviour, it is sometimes convenient to treat the subject as an aside, or a consideration. What we would argue is that ethics should be the staple of all wellbeing activity, thinking and creation. Ethics, or *moral philosophy*, is about right and wrong. Very rarely do we see any wellbeing as a wrong. As a branch of philosophy, ethics shares a great deal with wellbeing, its origins lying in the word *ethikos* – relating to one's character – and the word *ethos* – relating to habits and customs. Further linking to wellbeing, as a branch of philosophy ethics asks: what is the best way to live? This clearly resonates with questions about meaning and purpose in working life, which we often see in the wellbeing narrative. Larry Churchill asked us to think critically about moral value, again forging links with the wider wellbeing debate. It is incredibly important to ensure that employees have an understanding of their personal values and beliefs, and that the organisation realises how leaders within it influence the development of an ethical organisational culture. The strategic importance of strong ethical leadership cannot be underestimated, and the role of the leader is paramount to success. Organisations that promote ethical behaviour, prevent wrongdoing and have effective whistleblowing processes will undoubtedly create a workplace environment that is far more congruent with workplace wellbeing than those that do not. Research has also shown that fairness, respect and ethical behaviour have a positive impact on the public. We also know that fairness shapes the attitudes of employees, and that fairness also exceeds the expectations of most employees and can impact positively on productivity. Ethics and fairness are also 'teachable', and research suggests that organisations that do not conscientiously promote ethical behaviour have higher rates of sickness absence, presenteeism and general workplace disengagement. The literature on Organisational Justice and Procedural Fairness is quick to highlight this (Bradford et al., 2014).

Collective leadership

The notion of collective leadership first arose in comparisons with communism and the distributed style that emerged from that approach. Latterly, commentators have seen its worth when considering how much information is pouring into an organisation, and how leaders in that organisation manage it. There appears to be a consensus that there is too much for one person, or even a few people, to absorb, interpret and action in any meaningful way. Therefore, a collective approach is called for. In public services this may cause issues for the traditionally embedded heroic leadership styles that have adorned the corridors of power in days gone by. Here we instantly pick up on two very different approaches to leadership, one that is highly consensual and one that is very much command and control. To be clear, we suggest the latter cannot exist alongside authentic employee wellbeing and engagement approaches. We also suggest that it does not sit alongside leadership ethics and principles of ethical working life, as suggested by Nolan. Therefore, moves towards collective leadership approaches are a big deal for public services and impact significantly on the workforce wellbeing landscape. This new approach to 'power sharing' may be very difficult for some to consume, while to others it may be a case of 'about time'! We see these approaches playing out where areas of expertise in a particular area are called for and, grade aside, the best person for that business area makes the decision based on the evidence they have been educated or trained in or have subject expertise in. And what is more, the rest of the organisation will follow them, will trust them and will support their decisions. Followership is a key area of collective leadership. A further key area is the culture and engagement that need to accompany collective leadership. With origins in a supportive mindset, or growth mindset, it is easy to see the shift that may be required by some. However, this approach can provide huge rewards, for example by distributing work more evenly across an organisation, avoiding situations in which some have too much and some have too little. It is easy to draw in where the ethical components of working life now come into play. Collective leadership assumes a positive operating climate, which we know is beneficial to workforce wellbeing. If we take the moral philosophy high ground here, or the way we live our life, it is straightforward to connect the dots. One of the underpinning ethical constructs is that of trust, and leadership styles that invite openness and honesty as critical components evoke the trust of the workforce and lead to a far more conducive working environment, as we have mentioned in previous chapters. This also facilitates visioning and strategy communications in a far more coherent manner, listening and including employee voice. And whilst we are on an ethical vein, it is clear to see how notions of fairness and transparency are dealt with also. These strong ethical values really form the backbone of collective leadership, as well as dealing with the new working environment that many are faced with, as discussed earlier. Having the organisational maturity to create an environment in which employees can be involved in all aspects of the business, have a voice and are actively engaged in the success of the organisation, whatever that entails, seems to us at least to be the way forward.

4

WHAT RESEARCH TELLS US

Introduction

The aim of this chapter is to provide insight into what works, and what does not, in an attempt to guide and inform the reader from the previous chapter to the next; it is a conduit or bridging narrative. We explore the history of wellbeing, starting with its origins and earliest practical applications. We go on to explain the relevance of *keeping an eye* on the future workplace, and the massively changing face of modern day working life, proposing secondary and tertiary *industrial revolution* scales of change, the so-called fourth industrial revolution.

This chapter takes a brief look at stress, what the signs are and what and why people may experience workplace stress. More important, perhaps, is what managers can do, how they can help, what they need to look out for, and managing people back to work who have experienced a stressful episode.

We then move on to look at resilience training, and what that might include based on the resilience prescription (Southwick and Charney, 2012a). Best practice examples are illustrated, together with cautionary tales of errors in the field of operationalising wellbeing in the workplace. A balance of successful and less successful implementations is modelled in this chapter through case studies both here and (in further detail) in the final chapter. The subtleties between private and public sector programmes are explained, and practitioners need to be mindful that what works in one arena may well not be considered best practice in another; this is definitely not one size fits all! The context-sensitive world of wellbeing is unpacked, with a particular focus on employee relations and the differing common practices in both public sector and private. We propose that wellbeing cannot be delivered as the current management fad but needs to be part of the strategic planning process in any organisation serious about succeeding in these most challenging of times.

This chapter includes an overview of our work on leaveism, and what that says about the environments we create in the workplace. There is discussion of how this phenomenon plays out, what the implications are, and how managers can spot the signs of workplace stressors that may well lead to presenteeism and leaveism. We offer up a number of suggestions about how workers view their time in the workplace, and what can upset the balance. We suggest that managers who are skilled and sensitive in this area will reap the benefits in terms of both productivity and performance.

The chapter concludes with a glimpse at the likely future world of work, including commentary on flexible, remote and virtual working. What will the leadership look like in these environments? We also look at the evidence around the working populous, and in particular the ageing workforce and what the implications are for managers.

History of workplace wellbeing

The origins of the study of wellbeing undoubtedly stem from research on stress, which we have already touched on earlier in the book. The term can be traced back hundreds of years, but it seems that, until fairly recently, it has been largely eased into second place behind physical complaints. These are somewhat more obvious, seem acceptable in the workplace and are usually dealt with by process. This involves sustaining injury, diagnosis, treatment and recovery, followed by return to work as before the injury. What we would say is that mental health injuries, and it seems prudent to use that term for comparison, are not as straightforward to suffer, and even less so to diagnose, and treatment can be a lottery, with return to full capacity being questionable at least. However, we are of the opinion that, if treated correctly, recovery to full working duties is not only possible but probable if we take the appropriate steps.

It seems the original notion of workplace wellbeing, and we are distancing from medical health here to make the point, was introduced around the 1970s and began as an early occupational health arrangement, or a *worksite health promotion movement*, as noted by Reardon (1998). The objective was twofold: to relieve pressure on the healthcare system and to reduce the cost of sickness absence in the workplace by effectively shifting some of the responsibility onto the employer, in return for increased productivity and performance. Although a little 'finger in the air' at the time, evidence soon backed up this hypothesis and it progressed to the strategic significance the subject holds today in most organisations, and certainly most public sector organisations in the developed world. Early wellness programmes involved three aspects: awareness, lifestyle changes and environmental changes. This structure to some extent still holds firm. If we are to look at the notion of personal resilience as an example, awareness of what it is can be fundamental to making lifestyle changes based on individual character traits, and there may also need to be changes in the way one works, flexibly for example. If we put all these aspects into, say, a resilience training programme, one would expect things to improve, and evidence suggests this is so (Hesketh et al., 2015a).

FIGURE 4.1   Conceptualisation of wellbeing

It is interesting, and perhaps not entirely surprising, to note that wellbeing can be conceptualised in a number of ways. For the purpose of this book, we are happy with the concept that involves four sub-actors, as detailed in Figure 4.1. In essence, we posit that it contains elements of psychological, physiological, societal and financial wellbeing. Any four of these can act alone, or in any combination of the four, and result in our ability to cope being tested, i.e. our resilience. In other words, the stress of our experiences challenges our ability to cope. In terms of the public sector, it seems common to have a trigger, such as a financial change in terms and conditions of service, that then proceeds to kick-start one or all of the other three aspects, the perfect storm. We would not rank these either, for any one of them can, with equal effect, cause considerable harm to individuals that can result in workplace impact.

Stress

Work related stress is recognised as a major health issue in most organisations globally. Just as many award schemes, such as best employer, greatest places to work, investors in people, etc., examine how an employer treats and regards their employees, the issue of workplace stress can provide the perfect lens. This is because it looks at so many different aspects of the psychological contract a worker has with his or her employer. And as we have mentioned, the number of people leaving the workplace in the coming years far outstrips the number coming into the workplace. So it seems reasonable to assume that the workplace will need to be attractive, and not only in terms of fiscal contract. It seems that new generations hold lifestyle in higher regard than monetary reward, amplifying the need to get this right, especially in terms of highly skilled jobs. Workplaces where work related stress is found in abundance are unlikely to attract talent. Returning to a financial illustration to make this point as clear as we can, the Health and Safety Executive in the UK estimates that during 2015/16 some 11.7 million working days were lost to work related stress, which is 45% of all working days lost. Public services have the highest incidence rates (HSE, 2017).

It may be helpful to unpack just what stress is. Hans Selye, commonly referred to in matters of stress, offered up the notion that there were four types of stress:

1. Eustress – good stress
2. Distress – bad stress
3. Hyper stress – over-stress
4. Hypo stress – under-stress

Cooper, 2004

Now what immediately comes to mind here is that there are two groups of opposing descriptions, and Selye suggested a balance was required. In terms of workplace stressors, we can see here the first suggestions of work–life balance, rustout and burnout and other workplace phenomena, i.e. a balance between good stress and bad stress. For example, see Figure 3.2. A contemporary view is that some stress is actually good for us and that we each may have a 'set point' of what we can cope with. Obviously this may, throughout life, change considerably, but the notion seems to have stood up to scrutiny, and academics and scientists (or both) regularly look at how we can raise the bar in relation to this – what makes people resilient, in other words, which we discuss elsewhere within this book. We also know that people who experience stress deal with it in a variety of ways, and some of these are not particularly congruent with good general health. We commonly see excessive smoking as an indicator of increased stress and increased alcohol consumption, both of which can cause significant health risks in their own right.

So what exactly happens when we get stressed? There have been numerous scientific explanations and indeed entire books written on the subject. To simplify, chemicals are released in the body in reaction to something the brain perceives. In the animal kingdom this is simplified as preparing for 'fight or flight' (cardiovascular response, acute stress response or hyper arousal), according to the seminal work of Harvard Professor Walter Cannon (1915). The body's sympathetic nervous system stimulates the adrenal glands, which in turn trigger the release of chemicals like adrenaline and noradrenaline. This is what causes the increase in heart rate, blood pressure and breathing. But it seems this can occur when there may be no actual threat at all, and we (humans) can become stressed by just thinking about something, and that something may not be reality at all, i.e. no threat to our safety or welfare. So-called *thinking errors* can be very stressful, releasing these same chemicals in the body that make us experience uncomfortable feelings which can on occasion be almost unbearable. When you consider that it can take the body about an hour to return to normal, it is not difficult to see the long-term problems that constant exposure can have. Shelley Taylor suggested that female responses may not be the same as those of their male counterparts, positing that females may react with a 'tending and befriending' response (Taylor et al., 2000). That is to say that females may feel an overwhelming instinct to look after their offspring and seek security in groups. Instantly we can see that if neither of these options is possible, additional stress may be experienced. Unfortunately these cardiovascular responses can be very damaging, leading to cardiovascular disease. In simple terms, the heart wears out after repeated exposure to chronic high blood pressure caused by stress. To make things worse, once the heart has been damaged, it seems it is prone to both physical and psychological stress, and although medicine has come a long way, it is still one of the biggest causes of premature death, especially in males.

One of the largest studies in the UK civil service is known as the Whitehall Studies (Marmot, 1999), which looked at the impact of working over a lifetime and involved around 28,000 people over a 40-year period. The study was broadly focused on hierarchical position within the civil service and the social determinants of health, including mortality rates. The initial findings suggested that the higher up the organisational ladder an individual worked, the better their general health was in terms of blood pressure, cardiovascular function and general fitness. The research suggested that these individuals cope with workplace stressors far better than their blue-collar counterparts, who often drank too much, smoked heavily and were overweight. These were linked to areas we have looked at elsewhere in this book, and included in surveys, such as role clarity, job satisfaction, working relationships and control factors. In support of our position in this book, Marmot suggested that social support mechanisms could mitigate these shortfalls in hierarchical position. Indeed, recent studies in this environment, which has been greatly affected by austerity measures within the UK civil service, have shown that even people occupying the very top positions can now be subject to a great deal of stress.

In his seminal research on stress Professor Robert Sapolsky, a neuroscientist from Stanford University in the US, has shown in both human and baboon societies that low social status is a major contributor to stress and stress-related illness:

> We are not getting our ulcers being chased by Saber-tooth tigers, we're inventing our social stressors—and if some baboons are good at dealing with this, we should be able to as well. Insofar as we're smart enough to have invented this stuff and stupid enough to fall for it, we have the potential to be wise enough to keep [these stressors] in perspective.
>
> *Sisgold, 2015 p.124*

His study of stress in non-human primates has resulted in fascinating insight into how human beings relate to this universal pressure. His book *Why Zebras Don't Get Ulcers* explains how we process trauma compared to the animal world, generally concluding that we do not handle or process stress very well; it is a fascinating read (Sapolsky, 2004).

So it does seem that training or awareness programmes can equip us with the knowledge at least to know ourselves better, and to be able to spot the signs when stress is creeping up on us. With resilience training we can also learn how to notice in others that things are not well. This is the premise of our leadership narrative in essence, and we argue that all leaders should have at least some input about the subject of resilience, in humans of course.

Resilience training

Getting the right balance between wellbeing and operational effectiveness is undoubtedly going to pay dividends. What we are sometimes faced with, however, is that some view it as being too nurturing, nanny state type arguments. With this in mind, best practice has to be context sensitive. That is, it has to cohere with the business at hand. It needs to accord with the organisation's values, ethics, strategy, mission, vision and so on. Wellbeing is not just about taking care of all your employees; it is much broader than that. It is about employees feeling close to the business, involved in it personally, having some sort of attachment. When you can instil those sorts of feelings and emotions in employees, it is usually a sign you have got the wellbeing strategy just about right. Those environmental issues are paramount, and sometimes not easy to achieve. A typical example in public services is that on occasion things are imposed (from central government maybe) that are out of the hands of local managers or executives – issues like pay and conditions, premises, recruitment and promotion policy, and such. These need to be carefully judged and navigated.

We suggest, and have written about this extensively, that, amongst other wellbeing interventions, organisations should introduce resilience training for their workforce. Resilience on a personal level can help employees spot the signs of stress, both in themselves and their colleagues. It can also assist them to work under pressure and bounce back from the workplace setbacks that exist in most occupations, and we mustn't assume all will be fine all of the time; far from it, we would suggest. In order to prepare employees for these challenges, resilience training courses can help in the understanding and responses to 'normal' workplace stressors.

As we have briefly touched on previously, and harking back to Sapolsky's work, humans tend to dwell on things, which in turn creates feelings of stress for them, so called *thinking errors*. These can have a huge impact on the interplay between mind and body and can put a strain on our personal resilience, especially if experienced over long periods of time. These thinking errors were the subject, in part, of the great work of Dr Steven Southwick and Dr Dennis Charney. Their book *Resilience: The Science of Mastering Life's Greatest Challenges* (Southwick and Charney, 2012a) researched prisoners of war and people involved with natural disasters and awful traumatic events. The book contains accounts from survivors of the tsunami, Holocaust and 9/11 and prisoners of war, as well as army Special Forces instructors. It scientifically examines how they processed the events and eventually moved on with their lives, in spite of some horrific memories of those events, and how they managed to do this. The book contains what Charney describes as a 'resilience prescription' which analyses ten areas to help people to deal with, or bounce back from, trauma and mental or physical stressors and so improve their personal resilience. We will now briefly discuss these elements, which in one way or another form the core of many resilience training programmes, and how, as they put it, individuals can *bend without breaking*.

Being optimistic is strongly related to resilience. A positive mindset, congruent with Seligman's approach (2003), can be a powerful tool when dealing with both day-to-day stressors, what we have previously called the drip-drip-drip, and significant traumatic life events, such as the death of a loved one. What is more, optimism can be learned, for example by using cognitive behaviour therapy, which is normally used to treat depression and PTSD. Although it is generally accepted that being optimistic is partly genetic, Charney himself noted that 'genes are not destiny'. Caution regarding optimism, or over-optimism, is advised in the aptly named paper 'Prozac Leadership' (Collinson, 2012), where being over-optimistic, or weirdly optimistic, may be seen in some quarters as simply too much – 'Pollyanna' optimism, as Charney notes. In this respect a person needs to face facts, not replace them with a fairy tale, and to be realistic about outcomes. We would bring your attention back to the leaders' impact on those they are charged with here, and ask you to consider how this would play out in your own particular circumstances.

A further aid to resilience can be found in cognitive flexibility, altering a stressful event's perceived value and meaningfulness. Often referred to as reframing, it is the ability to accept what has occurred, assimilate it and recover to a normal, or near normal, state. Again this can be learned. In his superb book *Black Box Thinking* (2015) Matthew Syed discusses the psychological and business benefits of what he terms as having a growth mindset, arguing that failures are essential for growth and learning and should be accepted, used and moved on from. Interestingly, Syed makes the point that several public sector functions are traditionally oriented towards post-incident internal investigations and apportioning blame, a so-called *blame culture*. He suggests, and we agree, that this is quite negative for a number of reasons, chiefly because very little learning comes out of the mistake owing to employees' propensity (in the face of what's coming) to clam up or close ranks when it comes to giving information freely and openly about what occurred. As alluded to by Kübler Ross, holding fort in the denial stage is of little benefit to anyone.

The ethical stance features next, and we have spoken in depth about ethics in the previous chapter of this book. Embracing your moral compass is how Charney phrases this aspect of resilience – developing a set of core beliefs that are personally unwavering. This accords with our earlier mentions of ensuring meaning and purpose in life. One could view this as the spiritual element of resilience (Smith et al., 2015), or what one holds true, belief, faith, religion and so on. Altruism is strongly and positively linked to this aspect of resilience and we would suggest is a major driver to public sector employ. Again this plays out in the links to having meaning and purpose in life (Ryff and Keyes, 1995). Having a mission or goal that involves helping other people (as in charity work) is a very good example of this.

Role models, mentors, coaches, peers and other cohorts of people can be beneficial to personal resilience. In terms of leadership it is often useful to try to unpack what exactly it is about him or her that makes you quite willing to follow.

We can learn a lot from role models, and they do not necessarily even have to work in the same environment. In fact, most people's initial role models are their parents, or other relatives. What a role model is is subjective and can change over time, but it is suggested that this too can improve personal resilience.

Returning to fight or flight once more, fear can be very stressful and may not be experienced in the same way by everyone. People can experience stress when attending large meetings, going in a lift, speaking at an event, having an interview. What is important, in Charney's resilience prescription, is that people face these fears and find ways in which to cope, especially if any of these events regularly feature in their day job. Facing your fears has been proven to impact positively on self-esteem. This leads nicely on to the next aspect, that of developing active coping mechanisms. These may include seeking social support, which is the next area that can improve resilience. To evidence this claim Charney provides the example of the *Stockdale Paradox*, referring to prisoners of war in Vietnam (Jim Stockdale) communicating with each other by tapping on the walls of their cells. We have discussed social support already in this book, and we see this as a key area of overall wellbeing, as illustrated in Figure 4.1. This can be especially powerful in public service, where identity and common purpose promote the forming of social networks.

One of the other aspects in Figure 4.1 is physiological wellbeing, which forms the basis of a further area proven to have a positive impact on personal resilience. Evidence has shown that physical exercise is linked to improvements in mood, cognition, our body's immune system and generally feeling good and healthy. As well as physical training, it is also suggested that one trains the brain, knowing how you function and building emotional intelligence, moral integrity and so on. The importance of sufficient sleep is also important in this regard. The final aspect of the resilience prescription involves playing to your signature strengths and doing what you enjoy and are good at. Many mindfulness proponents would call this 'living in the moment'.

Mindfulness is worth a quick mention here, as it is still, it seems, quite a contentious subject. However, the evidence base for the effectiveness of mindfulness practice is nevertheless receiving burgeoning attention. In his book *Mindfulness in Eight Weeks* (2014) Michael Chaskalson points out that US congressmen and UK politicians are vocal about the benefits of mindfulness. There are widely respected programmes available in schools for children and young adults, US marines build it into their training, top corporations offer training to employees, it is NICE approved (UK), and there are about 40 scientific peer-reviewed publications published on it every month. Therefore it seems worthy of inclusion in this book. There are two main mindfulness approaches that are popular, Mindfulness Based Stress Reduction (MBSR) and Mindfulness Based Cognitive Therapy (MBCT).

MBSR was developed by Professor Jon Kabat-Zinn and, as the name suggests, is aimed at reducing stress. MBSR is based on meditation and yoga techniques, advocating full body scanning with the goal of allowing the practitioner to let go, be focused on the here and now, and be non-judgemental. Kabat-Zinn began his clinic in 1979, at the University of Massachusetts, so it has been around for quite a while. The title of his book *Full Catastrophe Living: Using the Wisdom of Your Body and Mind to Face Stress, Pain and Illness* (Kabat-Zinn, 2013) encapsulates the essence of the technique.

MBCT is targeted at people with depression disorders and uses traditional CBT techniques alongside mindfulness strategies, such as meditation. As with Charney's observations, it is aimed at acceptance and awareness of how individuals process incoming information without overreacting or detaching. This technique is designed to help people become less self-critical and self-destructive and avoid constantly thinking in a negative frame.

To conclude this section we would suggest that resilience training not only helps on a personal basis but is also enormously helpful for the greater good of the workforce in general, in that it enables recipients of the training to spot the signs in others, congruent with our leadership approach outlined in Figure 3.1. As we have shown, generally speaking though not on all occasions, the content of these courses usually includes elements explaining how to process thoughts, thinking errors, strengths and weaknesses and to think positively about situations and workplace challenges, looking for opportunities rather than concentrating on the negative aspects. All of these, we suggest, are areas in which self-mastery (knowing yourself) can create effective and well-respected leaders that understand the impact they have on others.

Personality characteristics and coping styles can have a huge impact on personal stress responses. As many organisations have already realised, stress is a very serious problem for a number of reasons, some of which we have already discussed. The diagnosis and measurement of workplace stress have undoubtedly become more intricate, with technological advancements. We will discuss this in further detail in the next chapter of the book. What we can say here is that cognisance of individual qualities should be taken into account when assigning tasks, and employers should try to ensure workers are well suited to the job roles they are being asked to perform. Public sector restructures are a particularly sensitive area where this can emerge, so-called 'job slotting'. Employees can claim that they can do an unsuitable line of work with additional training and take this option rather than redundancy or grade reductions. Although these job transfers may be preferred by unions, in that they negate job losses in the short term, the personal impact that ensues when employees gain little or no meaning and purpose from their new role can be a source of high levels of stress. This is a suitable area at which to target resilience training, should you have limited resources, as these organisational responses can be very uncomfortable for both those involved and the surrounding workforce. It is a further area where managers may need to have difficult conversations regarding suitability and potentially unhealthy work for individuals. Occasionally managers may find themselves balancing the conflicting needs of legal entitlement with future mental health wellbeing, and research tells us that resilience training is an effective means of addressing some of these issues and improving workforce wellbeing.

Leaveism

We have mentioned it only in passing so far, but the phenomenon of leaveism is highly prevalent in public services and provides a contemporary example of putting research into practice, from our own experience. We've long been concerned about the impact of absenteeism and presenteeism on workers and workplaces. But our recent studies have uncovered this previously unidentified phenomenon that sits outside contemporary descriptions of absence behaviours and fills a lacuna in current thinking on workplace psychology. To explain fully, leaveism is when employees use allocated time off, such as annual leave entitlements, banked flexi-hours and re-rostered rest days, when they are in fact unwell and may be entitled to take sickness absence. The same term can also refer to working outside contracted hours, including when on holiday or on allocated days off, when an employee is well (fit for work) but overloaded and unable to manage their workload within the contracted hours. These leaveism behaviours are distinct from those categorised as 'absenteeism' or 'presenteeism', opening up a new opportunity to explore notions of abstractions from the workplace that are born out of being unwell (sick) or unfit to perform to the requirements of the particular task because of stressors such as work overload, and where an employee may normally be entitled to time off sick. This overload work may be conducted when the employee is well but outside contracted (i.e. paid for) hours.

In our previous research, which took place in the UK police service, it seems that organisations largely ignore employees' need to complete work outside of hours or, indeed, effectively promote the practice through absence management policies and the effect that taking time off has on personal records. These effects, as discussed with other notions of workplace practice, may be real or perceptual. Workers may feel that taking sickness absence could taint their personal record, opportunities for promotion and advancement, training courses and so on. Or they may do it out of a sense of loyalty, commitment and other positive feelings towards the organisation. Although the reasons are yet to be fully understood, leaveism undoubtedly, and significantly, skews the true picture of workforce wellbeing. A recent police federation survey (in the UK) asked its members about the prevalence of leaveism. The responses ($n = 16,841$) revealed that 59% had taken annual leave or rest days to take time off due to being unwell through physical health on one or more occasions; 42% said they had taken annual leave or rest days to take time off due to being unwell through stress, low mood, anxiety or other problems associated with psychological health on one or more occasions; 50% of respondents conceded they had taken work home that they could not complete in normal working hours, and 40% stated they had taken work home whilst on annual leave that could not be completed in normal working hours (Houdmont and Elliott-Davies, 2017).

Furthermore, we know in some public sector organisations employees have a 'quota' of sickness, which, if exceeded (such as by taking three or more days off sick, or having three or more occasions of sickness absence within a set period), somehow reflects poor performance. Taking annual leave rather than sickness leave therefore makes a lot of sense to an employee who is worried about their perceived job performance. Here we refer to 'perceived' again, because this may not echo reality, although needless to say it is still as impactive on the individual concerned. Further research found that 76% of employees who have practised leaveism have done so to avoid being labelled as 'poor performers' or 'unable to cope' with their workload (Hesketh et al., 2014a). This may lead to sickness absence going under-reported by individual employees and distorts both the incidence of sickness in the workplace and the organisation's ability to understand and manage employee wellbeing.

We consider that the issue for most organisations is the impact that leaveism would have if it converted into sickness absence. A piece of research from Austria suggests that the 'fear of job loss' or 'downgrading' and 'low perceived job gratification' appear to increase the likelihood of leaveism occurring (Gerich, 2015). At a Health at Work conference in Birmingham, UK, a show of hands revealed that almost all the audience (of public and private sector organisations) had experience of leaveism in their own workplaces. We note that presenteeism is on the rise too. In the CIPD's latest Absence Management report (2015), a third of all organisations reported an increase in people coming to work ill in the previous 12 months. Such an increase is more likely in companies where long working hours are seen to be the norm and where operational demands take precedence over employee wellbeing. The organisations that reported a rise in presenteeism are nearly twice as likely to report an increase in stress-related absence, and more than twice as likely to report an increase in mental health problems. Worryingly, nearly three fifths (56%) of organisations that have noticed an increase in presenteeism have not taken any steps to discourage it. Although we have no data as yet on leaveism, we would suggest that there would be a similar picture?

The motivations behind leaveism are, at this stage, not entirely clear and appear to differ from case to case. We are carrying out further research to establish what exactly drives these reactions to workplace workload and ill health. It does seem an employee may come to work ill, or take annual leave to recover from illness, simply because they need the money and cannot financially afford to take time off sick. Or they could be taking work home that cannot be completed in contracted hours. We suggest that actually leaveism could even be triggered by a combination of both of these. In these cases, leaveism could be considered an act of 'organisational citizenship', leaving us to consider whether leaveism should be viewed through a positive or negative lens. This poses several unanswered questions, and our future research will look to establish explanations for the leaveism phenomenon, such as if it extends to people with a caring responsibility for young and/or old people? Are workers using time off to rest and recuperate? Or are they using the time to take on potentially emotionally challenging domestic roles? How does this all impact on the workplace?

Both the public and the private sectors are currently facing a whole host of challenges, from austerity and technological uncertainty to the presence of a three-generation workforce. Employee wellbeing, it could be argued, has never been so important in ensuring sustainable performance. Understanding employee behaviours is key to getting this right, so organisations should be mindful of the leaveism phenomenon and have a strategy in place to mitigate the consequences of its potential conversion into sickness absence. Should this occur, which we suggest may come about in response to a breakdown in the psychological contract between an employee and employer, causing them to become disengaged with the workplace, the sickness rates could soar dramatically or productivity could noticeably decrease? As illustrated in the research above, in terms of the sheer percentages of the workforce admitting to the practice, it is not to be ignored. As an illustration of the impact, poor health and wellbeing, according to the CIPD, cost the UK economy up to £5 billion a year in lost productivity. The same report suggests that healthy, highly engaged employees are productive by up to an average of 30 days more (RAND Europe's Survey for Vitality Health on Britain's Healthiest Workplace, 2016).

A glimpse at the future

The future is undoubtedly going to be technology driven, some referring to this as the fourth industrial revolution. We have witnessed exponential growth in developments in areas such as biotechnology, robotics, nanotechnology and artificial intelligence. It is difficult to imagine what the home will look like in just ten years' time, let alone the workplace. We already see gadgetry that can do just about every conceivable function and technologies that predict our behaviours, buying trends, health, lifestyle and so on. This fast-paced growth and utilisation is almost breath-taking, and how it is all going to impact on the workforce is largely unknown. What may be known, and known well, is that the workforce is in no way going to resemble what it does today, and may need reskilling and up-skilling to address the new work of tomorrow. What that skilling will look like is a further conundrum, and how we go about educating, assessing, promoting and developing our new workforce is also, to a large extent, up in the air. What we can say for sure, though, is that the central tenets of this book will be very much in demand, and that we will still need to create the right environment, whatever that may consist of. We will still need good and effective leaders. We will, more than ever it seems, need to draw on personal resilience as we rise to the new world challenges. Although this may seem a little space age, it is hard to imagine that the first computer link was only made in 1969, and the World Wide Web began in just 1989! Sir Tim Berners-Lee, then a 34-year-old physics graduate working as a software engineer, wrote a paper simply entitled 'Information Management: A Proposal'. Another way of looking at this may be that estimates predict that 65% of children in primary schools today will end up doing jobs that have not yet been invented. On the flip side, some jobs may well become extinct as technology takes over and can do the work 24/7 relentlessly and at less cost, making the traditional human elements redundant.

In a recent World Economic Forum report (WEF, 2017) there is a debate about what all this will involve in the way of moral dilemmas. Will this future world require a new set of ethical guidelines? Well undoubtedly the answer is yes – the ethics of artificial intelligence, robotics and things that have yet to be named will take some debating. These areas of work offer a whole new opportunity for workers skilled in entirely different professions to become extremely valuable to organisations. We have already witnessed this across public services, especially with administration and accounting functions. However, whilst technological advances create and offer huge opportunities in the workplace, they can also pose equally challenging threats to livelihoods, individual wellbeing and working relationships. These are not just the concern of public services of course, but of all organisations, governments and societies at large. We will just say a little more about two of these issues, those of leadership and IT.

In terms of leadership, we have written a lot already about what the future may hold for public sector workers. The landscape is far from clear, and notions of what makes good virtual leadership, effective remote working, flexi-time arrangements, work–life integration in a digital era and multi-generational workplaces have all yet to be fully explored. It is safe to say the nature of work is changing both quickly and radically. The nature of the employee relationship is also changing in public services. The biggest change is probably in the form of the state pension arrangements, where previously the course of working life would be fairly well mapped out and, barring any intervening catastrophe, it was more or less cradle to grave at the same place of employment. This is no longer on offer for employees, yet Gallup reported in the US in January 2015 that 30% of the working population was willing to do all they could to enable their organisation to succeed. Therefore there is still clearly a psychological contract firmly in place between most employees and their employers.

Technology also plays a critical role in delivering more efficient services in the public sector. One of the problems faced by public services is to keep up with the latest developments and the constant updating and upgrading of both hardware and software, all of which is extremely expensive. Choosing the right platforms is no easy task and can be a big source of stress to those charged with commissioning and running IT services in the public sector. For public sector 'users', technology can also be a source of stress. We have spoken about an ageing workforce, and there remain employees who will have had no experience of computerised systems *at all* until their adult life. This fact alone seems barely comprehensible given what we have seen develop in such a short space of time, presenting significant challenges in the workplace. The transformative role technology will play in future public sector delivery is simply eye-wateringly complicated, and with seemingly little central direction in most countries it seems we have yet to scratch the surface. Emergency services in the UK provide a vivid example of this, with little or no central procurement and no preferred systems being used or recommended by government. Yet the general public have an expectation that they should be able to access public services immediately, online, via their mobiles and utilising the latest gadgetry available. The digitally engaged public's thirst for the latest approach to service provision is something that certainly needs to be at the forefront for public service executives.

It would be remiss at this point not to mention the impact of social media on workplace wellbeing. We now have a situation where managers can both transmit and receive key messages to a global audience in live time. This can be both helpful and also unforgiving. The public thirst for information about a whole range of public authority work is insatiable. On top of this, where there is no information forthcoming, there are commentators aligned to fill in the gaps with so-called fake news. This can be a huge source of stress for those charged with leading people, and very often conflicting needs are presented for resolution, which again can be a big source of stress. The speed at which managers have to consume, analyse and make decisions based on that information is an area that many managers find very challenging. However, with the speed and volume of information transfer increasing all the time, this is unlikely to get any better and is an area where leaders in all walks of life will need to up-skill or reskill.

5

APPLYING RESEARCH IN YOUR WORKPLACE

Best praxis

Introduction

This penultimate chapter looks at how to put the information, skills, research and evidence from the previous chapters into action in the workplace – praxis. It picks up from the previous debate and explores what successful wellbeing may look like in the workplace, based on the practical knowledge and experiences gained by others, many of whom are corporate giants. Evidence-based advice on how to monitor, update, horizon scan and evaluate wellbeing programmes is provided in vivid detail, along with suggestions for application based on empirical evidence. The reader should thus be equipped with a definitive idea about how wellbeing will look and perform in their own organisation, and how to confidently weave it into an already complex business setting.

The factors that affect mental health are many, but in terms of research we can break them down into components that provide personal triggers for poor mental health. Under normal circumstances, the most immediate factor is the death of someone who is very close to you. Unfortunately this is inevitable for almost all of us, and is well researched in terms of what happens psychologically; see, for example, the grievance cycle in Figure 5.1. It is also extremely important to understand what we can do to cope with this awful time in our life. In terms of work, the threat of redundancy or job uncertainty can place us in a low state and will often trigger other wellbeing concerns, including societal and financial, resulting in a tsunami of worry and stress.

There are numerous other issues that can also impact on our working life, and in this chapter we will look at how you can apply an abundance of research to construct a framework for managing, monitoring and evaluating wellbeing in the workplace, and how you can implement wellbeing in your workplace by creating a wellbeing framework. We will go on to explain how to monitor, update and evaluate your chosen approach and what to look out for. These practical recommendations should be considered together with some of the case studies provided in the following chapter. These detail how the plans may work out in the workplace, giving you a close look at the benefits and the occasional pitfalls to watch out for. We hope that this very practically oriented section will be of great use to academics, practitioners and those in training alike. The approach should always be viewed as cyclical, and to get the best out of any strategy it is best to set review periods in which to monitor, adjust and refresh in the light of any emergent issues, legislation or best practice examples from elsewhere. This maturity is what will ultimately pay dividends.

Grievance or change cycle

We feel it to be prudent to briefly introduce and explore a seminal piece of work, the grief cycle. What goes on when people experience events that knock them off balance (with the thought in mind that we will all experience this at some point in our lives)? One of the best-known models that address this is the grievance cycle model. Dr Elisabeth Kübler-Ross, a Swiss-American psychiatrist who pioneered methods in the support and counselling of people who had experienced personal trauma, grief and grieving, associated with death and dying, conceived this model, writing about it in her book of 1969 *On Death and Dying*. She also dramatically improved the understanding and practices in relation to bereavement and hospice care. Her ideas, notably the grievance model depicted in Figure 5.1, which we will talk through shortly, are transferable to personal change and emotional upset resulting from factors other than just death and dying. Many business commentators, academics, consultants and practitioners have found the cycle helpful in understanding, explaining and dealing with a host of psychological conundrums. These

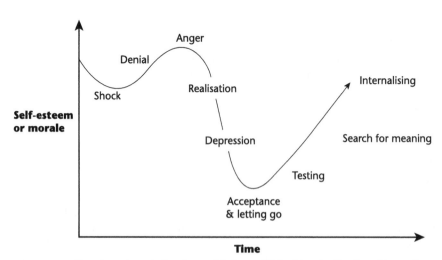

FIGURE 5.1 Based on the grief cycle model first published in *On Death and Dying* by Elisabeth Kübler-Ross, 1969

include relationship problems, drug and alcohol addiction, workplace change programmes, major health issues, money problems and so on. What can also be seen, as you work through the model, is that it can be applied to relatively minor, but nevertheless stressful, situations, which have the potential to blow up if not dealt with, or diffused, effectively. In this case we suggest that the model can also be applied, by skilful managers, in situations that are not life threatening or even serious in themselves. Some valued employees require a dynamic intervention to prevent a drip-drip-drip effect becoming an issue, such issues including overtime, promotion, minor disputes with colleagues, time off and so on. The stages illustrated in Figure 5.1 are further explained below, though note that the original concept involved only the five stages of *denial, anger, bargaining, depression* and *acceptance*.

Stage 1 – Shock and surprise at the event or announcement. This can be common when experiencing bad news. For managers, preparing people for this can go some way towards easing the impact of an initial announcement. In terms of change announcements, these should always be undertaken with empathy and with consideration for those who are going to be impacted on the most.

Stage 2 – Denial of the change and finding ways to convince yourself and others that it isn't really happening. It can be an awful experience for many people, and in a fast-moving working environment it can be eye-watering. Our look at thinking errors and cognitive reasoning should help people to get over this hurdle quickly. To dwell here is to suffer immensely, and with futility. Very often there is simply nothing one can do. Draw on the saying 'control the controllable'; if there is simply no control to be had, get out of there!

Stage 3 – Frustration on the way down and experiencing anger, often accompanied by a tendency to blame others and lash out. If there is no acceptance of the change, it is unlikely people can move on; remembering this is a cycle, it is not suggested you can skip stages, and the mind must process all these feelings, unpleasant though they may be. Our ability to move through the gears is what is vital here.

Stage 4 – Depression. Hitting rock bottom and experiencing depression and apathy. Everything seems pointless and purposeless. A lack of self-confidence may creep in. Most commentators agree this is the critical juncture that people need to exit as soon as is feasible. It can be very difficult to move on from. Lots of social support, care, empathy and motivation are required from those around.

Stage 5 – Experimentation. This is where people who haven't given up entirely and opted out of the process start to experiment with the new situation and try new things out. Again, a circle of support can greatly assist in this area – someone to talk to, to listen, to understand what they may be going through – and attempts to move on.

Stage 6 – Deciding what works and what doesn't. Coming to terms with what's happened and beginning to feel more optimistic and positive. This is very often the point where people declare to themselves that the stage is over and it is time to get on with things. Social support is still needed to avoid relapse, but here things start to look a lot more optimistic.

Stage 7 – Integrating the change into life so it becomes part of the way things are now done. Very much emerging from the other side, conceding life will not be the same again, but having come to some peace that it can continue, not quite where it left off, but nonetheless it is well and truly behind us.

Taking this out of its original context, we can clearly observe similar reactions to those described by Kübler-Ross's grief model in people confronted with far less serious traumas than death and bereavement, such as redundancy, enforced relocation, crime and punishment, disability and injury, relationship break-up, financial despair and bankruptcy, etc. This is why the model is so relevant to the wellbeing approach and what makes it worthy of study and reference far outside the context of death and bereavement. We can actually view the 'grief cycle' as a 'change model' for helping to understand and deal with (and counsel via occupational health type services if needed) personal reactions to traumatic events. These traumatic events are viewed through the lens of the person undergoing them, notwithstanding they may not be seen as traumatic at all by others. Trauma and emotional shock are relative in terms of their effect on people. While death and dying are for many people the ultimate trauma, people can experience similar emotional upsets when dealing with many of life's challenges, especially if confronting something difficult for the first time and/or if the challenge happens to threaten an area of psychological weakness, which we all possess in different ways. One person's despair (changes at work in our case) is, to another person, not threatening at all. Emotional response, and trauma, must be seen in relative not absolute terms. The model helps remind us that the other person's perspective is different from our own, whether we are the one in shock or the one helping another to deal with their upset. The role of managers here, as is probably blatantly obvious, is both to recognise the signs that this is what their people are feeling and experiencing and to have the skills and abilities to help them through it, quickly and effectively. Great managers do this really well.

We suggest that although many of these events may well occur in isolation, unfortunately they can also come in one huge wave of upset and trauma. Social isolation can result if left unchecked, and this can be a trigger for serious emotional ill health (e.g. PTSD). Indeed this features as one of our four aspects (sociological) that make up overall wellbeing, as depicted in Figure 4.1 earlier in the book.

As can be seen, many of these events overlap, and managers may find themselves not only experiencing some of these problems but also being charged with looking out for signs in the workplace. An example is child abuse or, as it has recently been labelled, adverse childhood experiences, which can result in later-life mental health problems. This book is aimed at trying to reduce the huge burden of the task facing leaders, or at least outlining how mechanisms can be put in place for effectively addressing the issues as and when they inevitably arise.

Another of our four descriptors is that of financial wellbeing, or money worries in its simplest form. These can be both short and long term and can be dependent on the next aspect, which is caring for a family member or a friend. We now live, as we will explore in a little more depth later, in the time of a so-called sandwich generation, where we may find ourselves looking after younger children and older relatives or friends at the same point in time. Both of these heavily dependent responsibilities can be emotionally and financially draining. This drain can also lead, in a domino type effect, to relationship issues that can be sparked by a number of things: reduced time with loved ones, more hours at work, school runs, hospital runs, treatments, juggling work, less room in the house and so on. With most health services preferring community treatments, the onus has shifted on to carers to transport the infirm from appointment to appointment, which can eat massively into work–life balance.

And finally we move to psychological wellbeing triggered by workplace issues. We include this list to illustrate the fact that psychological triggers can have many modes, and multi-modes. The workplace is but one of these and can sit in the complexity of other 'stuff' that makes up the human being. So although the workplace is an important consideration for the mental health of the workforce, managers need to take into account external factors also if they are to truly understand their people.

Implementing wellbeing

There are many government wellbeing schemes or initiatives that provide information on what to do, suggestions of best practice and so on. For example, in the UK the National Institute for Health and Care Excellence (NICE) issues periodic advice and guidance documents for the public and consumers of health and care, a population with far too many offshoots to even attempt to categorise. NICE have recently (2017) issued guidance on what a healthy workplace may look like and contain. They have broken down their advice into four key themes, which they relate as *statements*:

Statement 1 – Employees work in organisations that have a named senior manager who makes employee health and wellbeing a core priority.

Statement 2 – Employees are managed by people who support their health and wellbeing.

Statement 3 – Employees are managed by people who are trained to recognise and support them when they are experiencing stress.

Statement 4 – Employees have the opportunity to contribute to decision-making through staff engagement forums.

NICE, 2017

As we have suggested, once you have the right leaders and managers in place, ones that understand people and people issues, we would suggest you are more than already on the road to creating the right working environment for your people. However, keeping up with the latest guidance is still important. In the UK many public services access the Workplace Wellbeing Charter (Black, 2015), a predecessor of the public health responsibility deal, which is essentially a set of standards, along with a self-assessment framework, that organisations can work to. Frameworks are a really helpful way of reviewing what your organisation has in place (or doesn't have in place) in relation to employee wellbeing. They can then be used to inform a simple strategy, or to form part of a larger organisational plan. The opportunity to obtain an independent assessment, comparing the organisational view of what is in existence to that of an outside body, can be particularly useful in reality testing, and we see similar schemes available in many countries around the globe, for example the World Health Organization's Healthy Workplace Framework and Model (Burton, 2010), and the Centers for Disease Control and Prevention (2016) model which looks at four stages, Assessment, Planning and Management, Implementation, and Evaluation (2016), to govern and monitor workplace wellbeing.

These schemes can be a really good starting point for any employer and can be delivered at relatively low (or no) cost, and we suggest they provide a good investment in terms of both time and money. The positive impact a structured approach to wellbeing can have on all staff can help improve productivity, performance and workplace attitudes. As we have alluded to earlier, attitudes and perceptions about the workplace are really important to improve workplace wellbeing. Once the basic aspects are understood, one can look at a more detailed plan specific to one's own workplace.

To illustrate this, we have developed frameworks that look at so-called *blue light services*, that is, emergency services personnel. We will provide a brief example here. These frameworks include advice, guidance and the signposting of wellbeing issues that are pertinent to blue light workers, but that may not be relevant to the general working population. If we take policing as an example, one of the issues police officers are exposed to is physical violence. Whilst in other occupations this may be completely unacceptable, in policing it could be considered 'part of the job'. As such, strategies need to be developed to enable police officers to cope when physical violence, as it inevitably will, occurs. These frameworks outline coping mechanisms, as in resilience, to manage the physical and psychological impacts, which may involve being adequately trained in defensive tactics and ensuring officers have the right equipment and are trained to use it. Regular training, familiarity and conditioning are known to help officers enormously when it comes to dealing with being assaulted, and many advancements have emerged from lessons learned in respect of this.

Although this may seem like a rather dramatic example with which to illustrate how preparedness can help staff deal with psychological trauma, it does clarify that, almost whatever the circumstance in the workplace, a well thought out evidence-based approach can help mitigate the effects of lowered levels of psychological and physiological wellbeing.

Creating a framework

We now move on to the very practical elements of this book and ask: what would a wellbeing framework contain? We would suggest that you orient towards the generic workplace factors, many of which we have covered already in this book, with bespoke or nuanced items that are pertinent to the business of the organisation that is the subject of the framework. Our experience tells us that, in the case of public services, many of the basics are legislated for under health and safety at work policies and so on, whatever these may look like in the many different countries around the globe. A framework ought to acknowledge this, but also take care not to simply regurgitate legislation. The workforce want most of all to know that they are being acknowledged as a valuable asset and essential to the success of whatever it is the organisation provides or does for their publics. The drivers may be very different from those in the private sector, especially in terms of financial reward. Bureaucracy can be a large source of stress in public services, so the last thing you want to do is make things more stressful by introducing lots of onerous activities and reporting mechanisms; that isn't very wellbeing! Also, any framework you create needs to be monitored, and we will speak more of that in the following section. Needless to say, you need to be able to track progress and know that your interventions are having the desired effects and improving wellbeing for your employees; an evaluation loop of some sort can achieve this.

We will return to the example of the framework that was used for policing in the UK, and which is set out in Table 5.1, with each heading containing a number of items for the subject police force to consider. The considerations involved a self-assessment, i.e. how well they are doing in relation to this particular point. This was simplified into a scoring percentage, letting those leading on wellbeing to self-assess and categorise their own performance. The categorisations for each of the items were *underdeveloped*, *being developed* or indeed *fully developed*.

Such tools can be really helpful, and of course quite subjective in nature. Once the focus is on the elements of each item, it is relatively simple to look at what is available to employees, and where there are clearly gaps that require addressing.

What there is no shortage of, it seems, is information on schemes and systems of addressing workplace wellbeing. The Internet has an abundance of ideas about good practice, and it is probably a good place to start to look at elements that would be congruent with the organisation the framework is being prepared for, and the wellbeing hazards that can exist in that particular line of business.

A brief example is provided in Table 5.1 to help get you thinking about what issues would exist within your own framework. What we would suggest is that you marry this up with any subsequent surveying you may wish to embark on. We have covered surveying in other areas of this book, but it is good to keep in mind how the issues will relate to each other as you progress. It is better to look at this as a continuous cycle, being regularly evaluated, tweaked and run again.

By way of example, if we look at the contents of the Absence Management item, here we would see probes about attendance management policy and how well

TABLE 5.1 A wellbeing framework example

Item
Absence Management
Leadership
Protecting the Workforce
Mental Health
Personal Resilience
Creating the Right Environment

employees know it, and what employees are entitled to, or even what is not allowed. Areas of contention in the public sector here can lie in compassionate time off, annual leave entitlements, sickness measurement and so on. This may lead on to considerations around the organisation's return to work (following a period of absence) procedures, including recording practices and information sharing protocols. Here we may also find items laying out the approach to psychological ill health monitoring and procedures, including reasonable adjustment policies, for example. In this area you may also wish to document how those charged with leadership responsibilities are trained and equipped to manage staff absence, and what their obligations are, and the role that they play. This may include documenting training sessions or running scenario work to gauge understanding. The list could go on, but we think the point is made that all this can be very helpful when managing wellbeing in the public sector. If needed, the cost of sickness absence is a stark reminder. According to Health and Safety Executive (HSE) figures in 2016, the cost of UK work-related sickness absence in 2014/15 was £9.3bn, and that was discounting long latency illness such as cancer. So, in the Absence Management part of your framework, if you wish to include one of course, are elements that seek to clarify what is acceptable, what the rules are and how you would be looked after if you were unwell – what the corporate stance is. This is also likely to impact on both organisational culture and the ethics strands that run through most public sector organisations. These considerations are made in open forum, which we know is good for engagement, and are permitted to be challenged and improved. They can also be tested internally and externally, something which we will discuss later.

Although we have touched on leadership previously, when looking at a framework to effectively strategise, it can include the following considerations. Probably one of the most important features is to ensure the leadership approach coheres with the wellbeing strategy, and probably as important is that the employees see this link and can connect with the approach. Documenting where and how these take shape is equally important and can also be helpful in terms of public service accountability. Consult with the workforce around what leadership is valued, how staff like to be led (although we appreciate it is not a consensus) and what they view as good leadership. As we have mentioned, leadership is quite a tricky business; it is complicated and relies on multiple relationships, which on occasion can conflict. Good leaders find ways to navigate through these difficulties and bring about workplace wellbeing and productivity seamlessly. This begins with the senior managers effectively buying in to the notion of wellbeing. We see an increase in the use of pledges and such like, whereby leaders commit to the wellbeing agenda on a formal basis. Documenting, recording, disseminating this to the wider workforce cannot be underestimated in terms of good practice. Time and time again we hear surveys reporting back on perceived poor communication, often by senior managers. If such commitment documents are formalised, it gives the workforce the confidence to proceed with initiatives to improve wellbeing, many of which are delivered via effective leadership.

An area that leaders at all levels can make a great difference to is in the reporting of bullying, which can take many forms. Overbearing behaviour, repeated tasking, intimidation, picking on individuals, these are all forms of workplace bullying. It has a huge impact on the workplace and can be very distressing for both individuals and groups of workers, as well as being bad for productivity. An area linked to that is around whistleblowing and effective policies that should be in place both to facilitate workplace complaints and to register grievances and deal with disciplinary issues. Research shows us time and time again that workplaces that foster an environment of openness and trust have a more resilient workforce and are viewed as great places to work. If this is the case, then effective policies to set the ground rules and deal with infringements are surely worth investing in.

Monitoring wellbeing

One of the most straightforward ways to monitor the wellbeing of the members of a workforce is simply to ask them. It seems the simplest of approaches, but we know many companies do not survey their workforce to find out how they feel about work. We would suggest this is a pretty awful state of affairs and something that should almost be mandatory for a public service, whose main objective of course is to serve the public. We would question how the public sector can deliver services without any idea of how the employees feel about work and themselves, and as such there is a duty of care to assess the psychosocial factors that contribute to workplace stress.

Organisations also need to find ways to monitor the wellbeing of all staff, and one way of doing this is through a model we developed called the General Analysis, Interventions and Needs (GAIN) pyramid, illustrated in Figure 5.2.

We developed this model to give organisations assistance when devising metrics to illustrate employee status in relation to wellbeing. To date it seems capturing people data, or data on the 'people fleet' as we called it in an academic paper (Hesketh and Cooper, 2017), is somewhat limited and highly transactional in nature. Traditionally HR departments in public services have captured data on sickness absence, leave entitlements, flexi-time and overtime, and so on. There is a strong undercurrent of compliance management running through all of these measures. A body of research claims that HR managers do not keep up to date with the academic

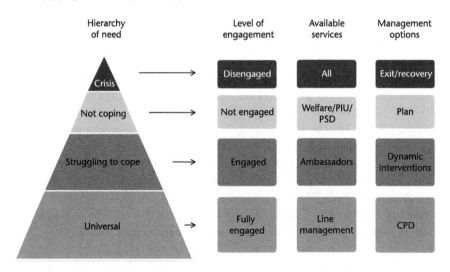

FIGURE 5.2   General Analysis, Interventions and Needs (GAIN) pyramid

literature being published, and neither do the consultants they subcontract various reviews to (Rynes et al., 2002). There is also the contested area around items such as the Bradford Scoring Index and other performance measurement tools that seem to pit Human Resource workers against the rest of the workforce on a regular basis, which is unhelpful and unhealthy. One of the areas we would suggest is given serious attention if adopting a tool such as the GAIN pyramid is to be very clear about who is going to use it and for what. Our intention is that it is used for positive mapping rather than in a punitive form. So if the intention is for the latter, can you call it something else please? As the saying goes, 'just because you can, doesn't always mean you should!' One of the key advantages of this model is that one can both see and acknowledge that from time to time employees will struggle to cope with the everyday work. This may be for a number of reasons, some of which may not have anything to do with work itself. This is where the 'struggling to cope' interventions are most impactive, and where decisive action can often improve employee wellbeing long before there is any disengagement at all. We think we are all entitled to an off day every now and then. Such lapses in commitment can be captured and dealt with quickly, if we know they are there, and if we have adequately trained and equipped staff to intervene quickly and effectively. This links to the leadership aspect discussed in Figure 3.1 earlier in the book. The 'level of engagement' aspect illustrates that although an employee may be struggling to cope, they may well be, and probably are, still engaged in the workplace. Here, phenomena such as presenteeism and leaveism can be observed by managers trained in the recognition of these features, and can form the basis of early intervention to assist their workers. What can be observed in many organisations is that the trigger for help and assistance is only activated once the employee becomes 'not engaged', when very often it is too late for a speedy resolution.

Another interesting way of gauging the wellbeing of the workforce is through the lens of others. Developmental peer review is one such approach to this, where an organisation invites experts, or people with relevant experience, reputation and skills in such work, to come in and have a look. This practice is increasingly used in the UK public sector and can be useful in establishing if, for example, a counter-wellbeing culture exists within the organisation. It all creates an effective means of employee engagement and, if well run, can offer an outlet for employees to discuss how they honestly feel about working in the organisation. The use of developmental peer review should always be used in a supportive manner; it should not be inspecto-rial in nature, should be non-judgemental and genuinely helpful to an organisation, to provide maximum value. Organisations that embed these practices report improved communications with their workforce and are acutely attuned to factors that impact on workplace wellbeing generally.

A further approach to workplace wellbeing is surveying. One survey instrument that we have both used extensively to monitor workforce wellbeing, and to establish other behavioural patterns, is called ASSET (A Short Stress Evaluation Tool). ASSET measures potential exposure to a range of common workplace stressors and assesses levels of physical health, psychological wellbeing, organisational commit-ment and, as we will now discuss, comparative data. Organisations and individuals can also use the findings from the survey, which takes the form of a self-reporting questionnaire, to benchmark their own performance against that of other organisa-tions and individuals, whether in a similar sector or not, and both public and private. In fact there are five distinguishing factors, with information on what we call the norm group available for comparison. These are:

1.   General Population
2.   Managerial and Professional
3.   Non-Managerial and Professional
4.   Private Sector
5.   Public Sector

ASSET, and of course other instruments like it, can be used to identify potential areas of risk within an organisation, and we have first-hand experience of using it as such with great effect. It is also useful for researchers, students and those tasked with HR work in that it provides evidence that is scientifically robust in support of workplace issues. One such example we can give was in the investigation and discovery of the leaveism phenomenon referred to in the previous chapter.

Evaluating and developing wellbeing

The ability of an organisation to look inwards and to see and understand what is going on in relation to their employees' wellbeing is critical. We would suggest that the public sector have a duty to look after their staff for both their benefit and the benefit of the public they ultimately serve, and who also pay their wages. Using frameworks such as the one we spoke about earlier, the Workplace Wellbeing Charter, those charged with the implementing guidance can monitor progress and evaluate what works in relation to their particular circumstances, and what requires improving. Now, we caution here that we are assuming it is, as they say, everybody's responsibility. But we would suggest that there is an identified 'lead' who can be responsible on behalf of the organisation and through whom is filtered the abundance of wellbeing information that enters a company, be it public or private sector. We also would recommend that the lead have a seat at the executive table, to report on this most important of people issues. As we have already stated, organisations that can should regularly survey their staff, to provide information on their progress and to track the general wellbeing of their employees. The use of maturity models can also assist, as can external reviews and other independent assessments. The main thing we would suggest is that organisations actively engage with wellbeing on an appropriate and sustainable level.

6

CASE STUDIES

Introduction

This will be perhaps the most interesting chapter of the book for those wishing to draw on practical experience at the highest levels of public service management. It concentrates on how those in charge have worked with wellbeing in the public sector and made enormous improvements in working practice. We believe nothing is better than practitioner voice for giving readers the confidence to take their learning into the workplace, drawing on both successful approaches and those that have been a little less so, or learning points as we may refer to them! We have invited various people to provide short case studies of good and questionable practice from a variety of public sector and private bodies, not only in the UK but in other countries as well. Discussions about the context, legalities and success are presented to allow readers to best place their own situational context, or future context for those studying, and find the best routes to success. We concentrate entirely on public services for the final chapter, with the majority giving examples from the caring sector, and the governance thereof. We have asked these contributors to provide heartfelt accounts, with the aim of informing the readers what their experiences actually were, even if this can sometimes read a little uncomfortably. This gives a fascinating insight, and a lens through which readers can assess how they might deliver the ideas set out in this book, practically, in their own workplace.

We will outline each account to make it easier to navigate through the final pages. The first account is from the chief constable of a medium-size police force in the UK, with about 6000 employees and covering an area of about 1.2 thousand square miles. With around 76% of his workforce engaged on the front line, and having seen a reduction in employee levels of around one fifth over the past six years, set against a population that has risen by 2%, Andy describes how he has been influential in embedding wellbeing within his workforce. He further describes his drive and commitment to see this happen across the UK policing network as national portfolio lead for wellbeing in the UK police service.

Rosanna Hunt provides the next insight from the National Health Service (UK) Horizons team. The team has a long history dating back to the beginning of the century. Rosanna charts her experiences leading this relatively small team, with a huge mission, in becoming a Community Interest Company (CIC). This change will facilitate a more stable, sustainable future for the Horizons team, making it accountable only to shareholders.

As any transition process causes stress and anxiety amongst team members, Rosanna describes how many of us have come to enter public service with previous experience of public sector reorganisations, and may have developed personal strategies of survival and resilience. She describes how, through her own work to build capability for change in the NHS, she actively seeks out others who have developed their own resilience strategies and who have helped to build energy for change in their own organisations. The Horizons team teach NHS staff, patients and other stakeholders to 'rock the boat but stay in it', and one of their mantras is 'Go for No!'

Moving to the opposite side of the globe, Janice Riegen, a clinical nurse specialist in the New Zealand health service, provides a vivid example of her own wellbeing journey. Taking a trip down memory lane, Janice explains her key influencers and how she values the working environment as being the key to successful organisational wellbeing. Notably Janice talks about her own work as part of a strategic group looking to set up workplace wellbeing across the organisation, and describes the step programme she and others used to carry this out.

Justin Varney is the national lead for wellbeing at Public Health England and gives an account of his experiences of wellbeing in the UK, and the management of such. Justin explains that for too many managers there seems to be a fundamental disconnection from the issue of workplace health and wellbeing, and why it is important for businesses and line managers. He goes on to suggest that for converts it seems obvious that a healthy workplace is essential to a healthy life, and for a large portion of this book we have endorsed that position. Leaning on data from his own organisation, Justin notes that in England over two thirds of adults are in employment and spend on average over a third of their waking hours over the week in the workplace. So investing in health has to happen during the working day; otherwise a third of the potential time for change and investment is wasted. He suggests that this is no different from the focus on schools as key spaces for investing and shaping children's behaviours, and poses the question as to why it should be any different for adults who are in many ways equally institutionalised in workplaces.

Tony Vickers-Byrne provides the finale with a 'from the heart' account of his time as HR director with Public Health England. In a very personal and reflective piece, Tony cautions of the pitfalls of young managers climbing the ladder and potentially leaving a wake of hardship behind them. He draws on his own experiences in a lifetime of work in the field.

Andy Rhodes

Chief Constable, Lancashire Constabulary (UK police)

Wellbeing – turning rhetoric into reality

A good friend of mine has spent most of his career supporting organisations to improve their performance, always finding common themes holding them back. Communication, leadership and culture regularly come back to bite the senior management where it hurts, the bottom line, and so he is never short of repeat business. However, he is frustrated at what he likes to call the 'knowing–doing gap'. His clients are educated people with tons of experience in their chosen field, so why then are they unable to turn theory into practice, feedback into action and their own rhetoric into reality for the workforce?

I think I have learnt why. I don't profess to have all the answers but what I am able to offer is a view from a senior leader who has spent over four years introducing well-being into policing locally and now nationally. My starting point is the research con-ducted by Ian Hesketh and Cary Cooper, who have created a wealth of information and guidance about 'what works', the evidence base. Policing is by its very nature 'high emotional labour' (Cooper) and presents a fascinating challenge when it comes to taking this evidence and translating it into action. Add to this my personal interest in behavioural science, coaching and personal development and surely I started my journey well equipped? I fear not and if it were not for being married to a psycho-therapist, I think my own resilience would have failed me and I'd have settled for less.

Here is the story so far, highlighting the key lessons I have learnt along the way to achieving what I believe is the holy grail of organisational success – a workplace where people don't simply survive . . . they thrive. We are only just starting this journey but I hope to help similarly committed leaders by giving them the reassurance and confidence to invest the necessary effort that is needed to embed wellbeing into their places of work.

The story starts five years ago as we (UK Police Service) started to gear up for the impact of austerity, not just the financial implications but also the changing nature of complex demands, particularly around vulnerable people. Added to this were the challenges to our legitimacy following the well-publicised failings of Saville, child sexual exploitation, Hillsborough and Plebgate, as well as the introduction of elected Police and Crime Commissioners. It was a very busy time.

The strengths of the police culture are its 'can-do' attitude and a tendency towards command and control (great in a crisis), but like any strengths they are a weakness when they simply don't fit the challenge. There's a great quote I read in a crisis management book advising 'don't just do something . . .stand there!' I like that and I think we did put some (although nowhere near enough) thought into our approach to change despite the urgency and pace.

I like systems thinking methodology for redesigning work; it makes perfect sense yet requires a 'ying' to its 'yang' in my view, simply because the purist approach can become overly concerned with the wiring diagram, which risks ignoring people.

I discussed our options with a few people and we decided to introduce wellbeing as our vehicle for people change, alongside systems thinking. My rationale was that systems thinking won't land without cultural shift and wellbeing won't land unless you address the systemic flaws affecting the workplace created by poorly designed work, failure demand and blame. I think this was a good call looking back because it was a statement of intent to our people that we wanted to place them at the centre of change. I don't regret this decision, but I do wish 'I knew then what I know now' because we immediately raised expectations without really understanding just what we had taken on.

The remainder of the story will focus on describing the lessons, learnt the hard way and still being learnt today. Many of these lessons are very personal, for leaders at every level to read and reflect on but not to worry about . . .it's normal to fail and to fail whilst daring greatly is a laudable leadership trait that too few senior folk possess in my view.

Lesson 1 – Understanding feelings

When Ian Hesketh and I set up the national wellbeing working group, we added in 'engagement' because of its importance in understanding what is affecting the feelings, emotions and therefore the behaviours of our people. Too often we judge each other on what we can see, without having positive regard for what is going on below the surface. We opened up an online engagement forum on day one and asked 'what does wellbeing mean to you?' The feedback was like an emotional tsunami and took us all by surprise, with over 10,000 hits in a week.

What was the source of this visceral employee voice? Shift working? Dealing with horrendous violence and trauma daily? None of these featured. Instead we were berated for our approach to performance, 'the reds and greens' binary culture of new public management that our staff told us had taken away from them their meaning and purpose in a job they loved. They demanded answers and they demanded change if we were serious about their wellbeing. For me this was a personal turning point where I felt compelled to admit I had been part of this bad practice; it had enabled me to progress and so I took responsibility and apologised for being wrong.

This was just the start of the leadership being held accountable for their motivations and their behaviours and has endured as a theme in our engagement work. If you want to understand what is really affecting your people, then listen without judging, respond with humility and take action when behaviours don't match up to the values you espouse. Otherwise don't bother trying to deliver on wellbeing; it's as simple as that.

The leadership lesson here is that wellbeing requires us to be humble, to accept we don't know everything and to take responsibility for our past sins. Wellbeing requires selflessness and genuine compassion. Don't try to fake these things.

Lesson 2 – Leadership capability

It's easy to think of capability as a transactional issue, especially in an organisational culture that values credibility and experience to such an extent that it's part of our personal identity. Too often this is allowed to overshadow the personal capabilities that can be found in great leaders who are genuinely committed to personal development and emotional intelligence. In a recent promotion process I inserted a question about emotional intelligence (EI), asking what we meant by it, why leaders need it and where you are with EI. Insightful responses came back.

Despite us promoting a leadership commitment to 'know your stuff, know your self and know your staff', quite a few candidates struggled with their answers almost as if this were a strange new language they had yet to master. Others, who were equally operationally proficient, talked freely with energy and passion about EI; 'if you want a people-focused organisation, you need leaders with emotional intelligence' came one reply. I couldn't agree more and I'll explain why.

Wellbeing is very personal; what affects yours doesn't necessarily affect mine. Work may not be the issue (I often find it isn't), yet work is a place where personal crises translate into poor performance, absenteeism, misconduct and even, sadly, break-down. Part of the leadership role is to be approachable, to listen without fixing so that we can spot signs early and support staff. To do this authentically requires a degree of emotional intelligence and really sharp support options. If you don't believe me, ask someone who has been on the receiving end of a wellbeing conversation with a manager who is doing it as if reading from a script . . .there is nothing worse. It's got to be genuine, honest, compassionate and personal. I make a rule of never delegating anything to someone unless I know they have the capability to do it well.

Early on we sensed there was a gap in EI capability as we looked for options to create the early intervention conversation, and so we sought out volunteers to take up the challenge. We attracted amazing people who wanted to help us change the way we treat each other and have since grown a network of wellbeing ambassadors, naturally high-EI people who had hitherto received little recognition for these strengths. Several of them came to talk at a CPD event and related anonymised case studies to the audience; you could hear a pin drop as we listened to the reality of how big organisations not only fail to deal with personal crises but actually make them worse.

My head tells me that getting better at early intervention pays dividends; it keeps the people at work and increases productivity and efficiency. My heart tells me we should be doing this for the right reasons. Policing is an incredibly tough job and those who spend their lives working in it deserve the very best environment we can create for them. Wellbeing is a safety issue. We spend millions of pounds on physical health and safety but a fraction of this on emotional and psychological safety. Wellbeing is a long overdue reinvestment in my view.

No organisation will have high EI by chance; we need to recruit for it, we need to promote people who are committed to developing it, and we need to develop leadership programmes that stimulate it. The leadership lesson here is to accept that Rome wasn't built in a day; people with low EI aren't bad people and with hard work it can be developed, BUT you have to see genuine commitment not learnt behaviours because these simply won't wash when it hits the workforce. Stop promoting people who think EI is something that doesn't apply to them; they keep bumbling around your organisation upsetting people and damage the credibility of your intent on wellbeing.

Lesson 3 – The wiring diagram

So far you could be forgiven for thinking that my story lacks a bit of precision. I think this is often the case when it comes to the high level statement on wellbeing disconnecting from the experiences of the very people it claims to serve. Why is this so? If there was one thing I would do differently on day one, it would be to pay massive attention to what I like to call 'the wiring diagram' . . . the policies and processes we create that are meant to improve how we work but often do the very opposite. There is a propensity in the public sector to put 'policy before people', make no mistake about it, and what's worse is most senior people don't even realise their negative impact . . . because they aren't listening.

To successfully understand these policies, which mostly originate in HR and Occupational Health ironically, you have to be able to open yourself up to hear the experiences and walk in the shoes of the people who are affected by them. I have dozens of awful anecdotes in this area, and I will often gratuitously pull one out of the bag if I feel my audience is losing concentration when persuading them of the benefits of wellbeing. Shock tactics usually work well, I find.

My advice is to go 'policy hunting' in the following highly emotive areas before making any grand statement on wellbeing. I wish I had. Half-pay decisions, ill-health pensions, compassionate leave, absence management and Force Medical Advisor decision-making, these are all things that apply to your people when they are on the back foot but are designed to tackle the small percentage of lazy people we don't want working for us. Sadly they achieve very little with the lazy people and cause huge damage to the good folk who are in need of support and compassion. They create enduring and damaging urban myths that permeate the workforce, resulting in a lack of trust in the wellbeing message. The people who work in these areas have an incredibly tough job, but they need to maintain compassion even with challenging people. It's their job. The leadership lesson here is to make it your business to intrude and challenge when it comes to situations where you feel the process has been put before the person, to redesign the services to recruit great people who care, and don't let the wiring diagram determine how you treat people. Only you should be setting that standard.

Lesson 4 – It's about people, stupid!

I love this saying but not as much as 'we asked for workers and they sent us human beings'. Really? This is the final lesson I've learnt almost too late, and it relates to the generally poorly understood area of organisational development (OD) – not design, we always do lots of that structural stuff without thinking!

Wellbeing IS an OD issue, in fact it is OD. This is because the ingredients required to make a really successful cake of wellbeing can be found in the people activities such as Learning and Development, HR, resource allocation, demand modelling, ICT, culture, innovation, leadership and the like. How work is arranged and how we treat each other . . . simple. Two sides of the same coin but often disparate activities working in silos instead of towards a common goal. This sums up all the previous lessons I have learnt because it's taken me four years to get my head around just how confused the wellbeing agenda can get unless these areas are all co-ordinated and ideally driven by the workforce themselves.

Be warned, once you start putting people at the centre of change, listening to their needs and aspirations, you can't go back to top-down autocracy. It's commit completely or don't bother and settle for average. When you are actively engaging with people to understand what makes them tick, the prize is worth the effort on so many fronts. Not only can you be more efficient by cutting out waste, but you will unlock difference and innovation as well as reduce risk.

Risk, I hear you say? Risk is what policing is all about and those nearest the work understand it far better than the decision-makers. Whether it be operational risk or reputational risk, the connection between wellbeing and the things that keep me awake at night can be found if you are prepared to look hard enough. For example, misconduct. Inside every misconduct event we can see missed opportunities where the problem could have been spotted, and it always relates back to a behavioural issue blocked by a cultural one. Misconduct should be about safeguarding our people, which means getting ahead of the curve if we see the tell-tale signs popping up in patterns of absenteeism, incivility, business interests, relationship breakdown and debt. You simply can't do this after the event. Recruiting people with the right values, training people to understand these indicators and developing leaders who intuitively 'get' wellbeing for the right reasons requires co-ordination of all the OD ingredients.

Our ultimate goal is to create a learning organisation and to do this we must connect the dots, something traditional top-down hierarchies militate against – something 'can-do' tendencies can stifle by removing time for reflection. OD as a practice will constantly challenge us to ask 'why?' before leaping into 'the what and the how'.

Final thoughts

It's quite humbling being asked to write about the wellbeing journey, and the health warning is that these are my experiences and shouldn't be taken as a 'four steps to success' type of airport bestseller. As you can see, I have made some huge mistakes and I am still restless for more change because there is so much more to do and such huge benefits to reap. For my father, work was about attrition, graft and self-sacrifice and I saw how work wreaked havoc on his mental and physical health. It doesn't have to be this way and the changing expectations of the workforce won't tolerate this attitude any more.

Wellbeing in policing can return us to where we always wanted to be, highly engaged in purposeful work aligned to our core values. Thriving and no longer just surviving.

Rosanna Hunt (PhD)

Horizons team, National Health Service (NHS), England

Prioritising wellbeing in times of significant organisational change

Our context

The work of the Horizons team has a long history dating back to the beginning of the century. Over this time, we have succeeded in surviving several reorganisations of the country's centrally funded NHS improvement bodies. Currently the small team of 12 Whole Time Equivalents is embarking on its biggest ever change: we are to become a Community Interest Company. This will facilitate a more stable, sustainable future, free from the threat of abolition at the flick of the ministerial pen and accountable only to our shareholders (which includes staff), our social cause and our balance sheet.

Any transition process causes stress and anxiety amongst team members. Many of us come with previous experience of public sector reorganisations and have developed personal strategies of survival and resilience. Indeed, through our work to build capability for change in the NHS, we actively seek out others who have developed their own resilience strategies and who have helped to build energy for change in their own organisations. We encourage people to step into difficult conversations, get diverse voices in the room and not to give up even when faced with resistance. We teach NHS staff, patients and other stakeholders to 'rock the boat but stay in it' and one of our mantras is 'Go for No!' This is some of the content of our free Massive Open Online Course 'The School for Health and Care Radicals' – delivered to a global audience every February. We also deliver training on personal and team resilience and provide social platforms for others to share how to build a culture of resilience within teams and how to develop personal resilience.

We quickly recognised that whilst our team continued to perform well on its objectives, our health and wellbeing would be at risk if tensions were allowed to manifest and grow. We decided to grasp the chance to apply our teachings to ourselves by assessing and analysing our energy for change in order to move on, define our own future and reinvigorate our energy. This is where our journey to prioritise our wellbeing began.

Assessing our energy gaps

Evidence suggests that five energies are vital for teams to be able to unite and tackle change and transition effectively:

1. social;
2. spiritual;
3. psychological;

4. physical;
5. intellectual.

Our research (Land et al., 2013) shows that many teams in the NHS pay more attention to the latter two energies at the expense of the former three. To redress this imbalance, it is important to do more to create a sense of solidarity, i.e. 'we are in this together' (social energy), to create a safe environment for team members to understand what the change means for their roles and positions in the team and to feel safe enough to step forward into those changes (psychological energy) and to create a sense of shared purpose for the future of the team built upon shared values (spiritual energy).

Our analysis of the team's energy for change using the SSPPI Energy Index © revealed that the team had low spiritual, social and psychological energies and a strong desire to increase them. There are two parts to the assessment: the first part consists of a psychometric profiling tool that is statistically validated and robust. The aggregated results provide an assessment of the team's energy for change which can be compared to that of other groups within the database, or the whole database of 1500 participants. The second part is a self-evaluation tool, used to tell us whether there are any gaps between current energy levels, preferred energy levels and perceived energy levels in the work environment. This is what our team results looked like:

Energy gaps

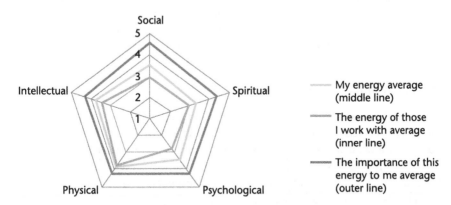

What this spider graph shows is that the biggest gap between current energy for change (the middle line) and desired energy for change (the outer line) is on psychological, social and spiritual energies. These energies are lower than the team would have liked them to be. Individuals within the group also evaluated the energy of those they work with (the inner line) to be lower (>1) than their own in all areas except physical energy. This is not an unusual finding and indicates that individuals have low awareness of the energies of those around them. By starting a discourse around energy for change, we knew that energy awareness could be improved for the team. We were clearly faced with the evidence that we just don't have a good enough understanding of what energises each other right now. Our research indicates that you can't start a social movement towards a shared future if you don't listen to and harness grass-roots energy. Effective, non-hierarchical conversations enable everyone to lead in co-creating the future.

There is a fundamental link between the use of the energy for change assessment tools and getting teams on a journey to develop a sense of collective agency, to become empowered to make practical changes and co-create the conditions that will help them to thrive during change implementation. We have seen this play out in over 100 teams we have supported through change. In our sessions with teams we often point out that anyone can bring negative energy into the room – it doesn't matter where you sit in the hierarchy, energy is equal and non-hierarchical. Therefore, it is not just the role of senior managers to model the change they want to see (for example, by valuing and trusting staff in order to build a culture of trust) – it is the job of everyone. Awareness of the five energies and how they influence our experiences is the first step to building a healthy, well team.

For example, a fearful environment (where there is low psychological energy) is characterised by tension between staff members, suspicions about personal motives and lack of trust. These experiences are personal and emotional, but because in our case the energy analysis showed how pervasive they were, the issues suddenly became valid. Responsibility for the issue moved from the individual to the team. We recognised that others also suffered from the stress that these issues were causing. This revelation was a major factor in the initiation of our wellbeing project.

Wellbeing improvement cycles

So far, we have conducted four 30-day wellbeing improvement cycles. These have focused on: exercise, taking breaks, email etiquette and kindness. Throughout each 30-day cycle we share research, ideas and inspiration via the Twitter and WhatsApp social platforms to co-create meaning and shared purpose amongst team members. For example, this week a colleague shared this inspirational quote about kindness using our team Wellbeing Twitter discussion group:

> If you are helping someone and expecting something in return, you are doing business not kindness.

We identified four parameters that an improvement cycle ought to operate within:

1. a simple team action;
2. possible to track daily and share;

3. everyone agrees with the action and encourages others to do it;
4. we do the action in work time.

So, with our first wellbeing cycle being exercise, we gave ourselves permission to do exercise in work time, whether this was going for a 5k run or having a walking meeting. We monitored our mileage and added it to a board in the office.

Using Survey Monkey, we measure team stress levels weekly, using a five-item online survey. It is not a validated questionnaire but it's quick, it helps us keep focused on what it is we need to improve, and it serves as a constant reminder that stress reduction is a priority for our team. The results are analysed in time for our Monday morning 'Huddle' – a standing meeting of the whole team where we put wellbeing at the top of our agenda – before discussing our work progress. We also allow a one-week break in between each 30-day improvement cycle to assess how successful the action was, and to allow time for reflection on what the next point of focus ought to be. Our external work is driven by assessing the evidence base and we wanted to apply the same thorough approach to our internal improvement effort. Several key insights provided the rationale for our work:

*   People in good health are up to 20% more productive than those in poor health (Emotional Resilience Toolkit, 2009).
*   Dame Carol Black's 2011 review of health at work found that investment in employee health and wellbeing is on the rise.
*   Stress is one of the biggest causes of employee absence (CIPD, 2008).
*   Organisations implementing major downsizing have 2.17 times the average sickness absence rates (Kivimäki et al., 2000).
*   Sickness rates are rising in the NHS. The average sickness absence rate for the NHS in England was 4.44% Jan.–Mar. 2015, an increase from the same period in 2014 (HSCIC, 2016).
*   Stress is caused by overactivation of the para-sympathetic nervous system (Harvard Health Publications, 2016).

Our research and subsequent action focused on four key wellbeing/resilience/stress-reducing factors:

1. exercise;
2. practising gratitude, kindness and compassion;
3. reduce multi-tasking and find focus;
4. activating the para-sympathetic nervous system.

Exercise is commonly linked to wellbeing at work, and recent BBC headlines suggesting that 'sitting is the new smoking' (www.bbc.co.uk/news/health-36411403) provided the impetus for us to start our wellbeing project with this simple action. Our research also revealed that taking a brisk walk shortly after feeling stressed not only deepens breathing but also helps relieve muscle tension.

Alongside our first 30-day improvement cycle on exercise, we erected a 'Team Appreciation' board in the office, which we used to stick up short notes on why we appreciated each member of the team.

Research on gratitude and wellbeing shows that gratitude improves physical and psychological health, by, for example, reducing toxic energy such as envy, frustration and regret, and increases happiness and reduces depression (Emmons and McCullough, 2003). Links between gratitude and stress reduction/resilience have also been identified. For example, Vietnam War veterans with higher levels of gratitude experienced lower rates of Post-Traumatic Stress Disorder (Kashdan et al., 2006). A 2003 study published in the *Journal of Personality and Social Psychology* also found that gratitude was a major contributor to resilience following the terrorist attacks on September 11 2001 (*Forbes* magazine, 2013).

Taking breaks in the working day was the focus of our second 30-day cycle. This was a concept that stimulated a lot of discussion between team members on our social platforms (Twitter and WhatsApp). We disagreed on what a good break actually looks like. However, we recognised some factors that impeded our ability to take proper breaks later and started to encourage each other to take breaks. Additionally we have co-created a list of stress-busters – team behaviours we felt would help to reduce our stress levels.

Future endeavours

We have noticed (from our weekly stress survey) that the team's stress oscillates over time and can be perceived as both positive and negative. Our interventions to date do not seem to have reduced the experience of stress, but our sickness rates have reduced from greater than 15% to less than 2% and energy gaps are diminishing, so our reactions to the stressors are more positive than they were previously. By equipping ourselves with the tools to manage stress (e.g. exercise, taking breaks), as well as raising awareness of the behaviours that can enable the team to function well (e.g. kindness, email etiquette), we hope, fundamentally, to create a healthy team.

We know that stress is caused by overactivation of the sympathetic nervous system and we plan to address this important factor in the coming months.

> The sympathetic nervous system functions like a gas pedal in a car. It triggers the fight-or-flight response, providing the body with a burst of energy so that it can respond to perceived dangers. The parasympathetic nervous system acts like a brake. It promotes the 'rest and digest' response that calms the body down after the danger has passed.
>
> *Harvard Health Publications, 2016*

Ashok Gupta, a co-presenter on our recent webinar on 'Individual and Team Resilience' for The Edge webinar series, has developed a free app that enables the activation of the parasympathetic nervous system via meditation, which some team members have chosen to use. We are also fortunate enough to have moved to offices with a prayer room, which provides a suitable environment for meditation practice during the working day. We know that meditation is an effective way to activate the relaxation response. Research uncovered by Ashok shows that Relaxation Response Training reduces anxiety and depression which are the third-highest cause of US health costs after heart disease and cancer – which also are affected by stress. In a study by Stahl et al. (2015), 4400 study participants had an average reduction of 43% in their use of healthcare services in the year after receiving Relaxation Response Training. Relaxation Response Training includes deep abdominal breathing, focus on a soothing word (such as 'peace' or 'calm'), visualisation of tranquil scenes, repetitive prayer, yoga and tai chi (Hartfiel et al., 2011). As a team, we will be learning more about how to activate the parasympathetic nervous system through regulation of the breathing in the coming weeks from Michael Townsend Williams, author of *Do Breathe*.

References

(All website URLs were accessed on 6 June 2017.)

Black, C. and Frost, D. (2011) *Health at work – an independent review of sickness absence*. Available at: www.gov.uk/government/uploads/system/uploads/attachment_data/file/181060/health-at-work.pdf.

CIPD (2008) 'Absence Management Survey Report'. Available at: www.cipd.co.uk/NR/rdonlyres/6D0CC654-1622-4445-8178-4A5E071B63EF/0/absencemanagementsurvey report2008.pdf

Emmons, R.A. and McCullough, M.E. (2003) 'Counting Blessings Versus Burdens: An Experimental Investigation of Gratitude and Subjective Well-Being in Daily Life', *Journal of Personality and Social Psychology*, 84(2), pp. 377–389.

Emotional Resilience Toolkit (2009) 'Healthy People = Healthy Profits'. Available at: www.bitc.org.uk/sites/default/files/emotional_resilience_toolkit_0.pdf

Forbes magazine (2013). Available at: www.forbes.com/sites/amymorin/2014/11/23/7-scientifically-proven-benefits-of-gratitude-that-will-motivate-you-to-give-thanks-year-round/#145a2cf56800

Hartfiel, N., Havenhand, J., Khalsa, S.B., Clarke, G. and Krayer, A. (2011) 'The Effectiveness of Yoga for the Improvement of Well-Being and Resilience to Stress in the Workplace', *Scandinavian Journal of Work, Environment and Health*, 37, pp. 70–76.

Harvard Health Publications (2016). Available at: www.health.harvard.edu/staying-healthy/understanding-the-stress-response

HSCIC (2016) Available at: www.hscic.gov.uk/catalogue/PUB17903

Kashdan, T., Uswatte, G. and Julian, T. (2006) 'Gratitude and Hedonic and Eudaimonic Well-Being in Vietnam War Veterans', *Behavior Research and Therapy*, 44, pp. 177–199.

Kivimäki, M., Vahtera, J., Pentti, J. and Ferrie, J.E. (2000) 'Factors Underlying the Effect of Organisational Downsizing on Health of Employees: Longitudinal Cohort Study', *BMJ*, 320, p. 971. Available at: www.bmj.com/content/320/7240/971.full.printest.

Land, M., Hex, N. and Bartlett, C. (2013) 'Building and Aligning Energy for Change: A Review of the Published and Grey Literature Initial Concept Testing and Development'. Available at: www.nhsiq.nhs.uk/media/2757735/building_and_aligning_energy_for_change_v2_feb_13_1_.pdf

Stahl, J., Dossett, M., LaJoie, S., Denninger, J., Mehta, D., Goldman, R., Fricchione, G. and Benson, H. (2015) 'Relaxation Response and Resiliency Training and Its Effect on Healthcare

Resource Utilization', *Journal Plos One*. Available at: http://journals.plos.org/plosone/article?id=10.1371/journal.pone.0140212

Rosanna works for the NHS Horizons team, which exists as a source of new trends, ideas, breakthroughs and knowledge in methods and mindsets for large-scale change, spread and improvement to help change happen more speedily and effectively. This is achieved by tuning in to and engaging with what is working in healthcare and other industries around the world, and by helping to build capability for change across the system.

Janice Riegen

Clinical Nurse Specialist, Occupational Health and Safety Service, New Zealand

My wellbeing journey

My story

Someone once called me a leader, but as I wasn't a manager, I doubted it. Maybe now I understand what leadership is, and so in some ways I am a leader, at least influencing others' thinking, starting conversations and hopefully inspiring others. So let's take you on the journey of what has shaped my personal interpretation of wellbeing in the workplace through working in a large public healthcare facility in New Zealand. I believe that healthy workplaces are the key to health and wellbeing in the workplace. They are about the health and wellbeing of individuals and organisations that have the ability to influence the health and wellbeing of society. We must use the evidence as well as keying into what individuals think and what suits organisations, as no one size fits all.

The beginning

Having been a general nurse for many years, one might think that the concept of well-being is normal, but not necessarily – caring is. How did I end up working in Occupational Health and Safety and when did the health and wellbeing begin to have a focus? Earlier on I went to north-west Australia to join my future husband in an iron-ore mining town. I ended up working in First Aid, attached to the Safety Department, and did a little health monitoring. Years down the track and back in NZ working in a large public health facility, I decided to have a go at playing badminton. An hour into this I injured my arm and then was off work for some time. I was introduced to Occupational Health and Safety as they helped me get some treatment and vocational rehabilitation. One thing led to another and the then manager asked me if I would be interested in working in the department. Closer to home, no shift work, school hours, how could I resist? It is because of her support and leadership that I am where I am now.

With all the legislative requirements, the focus was more safety than health. We talked about doing health promotion, but the work was usually so reactive. I joined the local Occupational Health Nurses (OHN) group and was persuaded to be a representative on the national executive group. This opened my eyes and I thought how OHN could be doing so much more. A colleague and I decided to present a talk at a primary healthcare nursing conference and we titled it 'The Forgotten Discipline of Primary Healthcare'. Searching for information, I found the work of Dame Carol Black and I was hooked. I attended a conference in the United Kingdom and had the privilege of meeting her the day before the release of the government's response to her report. This really was the pivotal point of focusing on health and wellbeing for me.

Most of my work was 'on the job learning', but I had started some academic studies, which was a whole new world to me. A few years on there was a new course for OHN with doctors; we were the guinea pigs! It was time to get some understanding of the theory behind the speciality. Did I think of health and wellbeing as critical? Probably not at the beginning, but what led from there has become my passion.

Large clinical service

A casual conversation with the head of nursing in one of our clinical services led me to being invited to do some work with them as part of a joint union/management forum engagement project. I started just after the World Health Organization (WHO) had released their 'healthy workplace' definition and action model – perfect timing, as this was then the foundation for our work.

What we did and how we did it

A steering group decided that 'face to face' engagement at a team level was the primary focus. The unions played a critical part and they identified four areas to pilot the work.

Stage one

Staff were encouraged to capture their views on healthy workplaces through an agreed set of questions, and ideas would be generated on how to incorporate these into their areas. We met with 47 separate teams and the participant groups varied in size from 4 to 28 staff, which resulted in over 560 participants out of a potential 1100. They included health professionals, health workers and administration staff. Inclusion of the union organiser in these meetings reinforced the message to staff that this was a partnership process.

We used the WHO 'healthy workplace' definition as a basis, with a quick overview of the evidence to support the work.

> A healthy workplace is one in which workers and managers collaborate to use a continual improvement process to protect and promote the health, safety and wellbeing of all workers and the sustainability of the workplace.
>
> WHO, 2010, p.8

This is a holistic, strategic quality improvement model that incorporates leadership, worker engagement, ethics and values at its heart and considers the physical and psychosocial work environment, what resources there are for workers and community engagement.

Originally we used the WHO definition of health, but staff did not align with this and we moved to the Māori wellbeing model: 'Te Whare Tapa Whā'. This is a framework which Māori use to articulate what 'health' is in their world. It is comprised of four cornerstones: te taha wairua (spiritual health); te taha hinengaro (psychological health); te taha tinana (physical health); and te taha whānau (social/family health). Whatever culture staff were, they related to this model and it had synergies with the WHO healthy workplace model.

What were our findings? Themes Through facilitated 'brainstorming' sessions, staff were asked what they thought made a healthy workplace at individual, team and organisational levels. This data was analysed through a general inductive approach and common themes were identified. All the work was typed up and fed directly back to the teams.

Two sets of themes emerged:

Personal health and wellbeing:
Healthy lifestyles; work–life balance; teamwork and personal responsibilities

Healthy workplaces:
Being: valued, supported and communicated with
Good: leadership, teamwork and job factors

Generally the sessions were well received with very positive feedback: 'it was really good to reflect and realise how well we are doing; I can't believe management really wants to know what we think; it should have been longer and it was the catalyst to start discussions in our team'. Contrarily, negative feedback was that managers shouldn't have been present.

Through this work key areas of focus were identified and led to the development of stage two.

Stage two

The steering group decided to extend the work and 'face to face' engagement was seen as critical. We visited 33 of the original 47 teams. This was to feed back the identified themes, to give updates on the evidence and to use the time for an educational focus. Larger groups were subdivided and 'brainstorming' was used to identify what were the components of a dream team and what was resilience for them. At the end there was an evaluation set of questions.

All of the teams related to the themes identified. Most of the teams identified that stage two was a valuable learning opportunity and was the chance for much needed 'team time'. The work was fed back to them, but the information collected has not been analysed.

There was some analysis through a set of evaluation questions. The results were surprising in that approximately 60% identified that since this work they had made changes in their own health and wellbeing. In addition many teams had gone on to work on culture change within and they found the work valuable. 'Thanks, this is an important topic; feedback from team great, appreciate energy and commitment to important area of health and wellbeing; highlighted that we know what is important, but need to work on it.' Alternatively, a few asked 'what was the point?', 'what will change?'

There were challenges and limitations to the work, but it was a 'snapshot' in time.

What were the recommendations? These were given under three main headings: leadership, engagement and teamwork. Each of these had tasks to achieve the recommendations with the expected outcomes. These were then aligned at organisational, team and individual levels using the themes.

This work led the way in our organisation and, for me personally, gave me an incredible foundation to my journey. The personal stories and statements helped fuel my knowledge base and was really the catalyst for a passion, or some would say obsession!

Masters of Health Science (MHSc) 'Examining Healthy Workplaces'

I thought that I might as well make this work useful and use it as part of my studies, and so began my additional journey of a MHSc. I was fortunate to find a supervisor who was interested already in 'caring for the carers' and was able to help build in the work as a qualitative audit as part of a research portfolio.

The more I read, the more I became addicted to the evidence from all areas. But I did sometimes question why they weren't connecting the dots? I was also fuelled by the increasing engagement of the work at a ground level, their stories, the findings and the encouragement to keep going to be their spokesperson at higher levels.

Through my research it was easy to determine that leadership was absolutely critical. Whether it was authentic, values based, compassionate or whatever, people had to be at the heart. One book that stood out in simple language for me was by Kouzes and Posner, *The Leadership Challenge*. Their five practices of leadership rang true: model the way; inspire a shared vision; challenge the process; enable others to act and encourage the heart.

Wider organisational group

I was supported to continue this work part-time in the wider organisation. Going into areas with no knowledge of the work was very different from being invited to participate and lead. So I started again, building up interest, going to business meetings and starting those conversations. At the end of the first year, I managed to get a steering group (inclusive of the main unions) together of interested leaders who had the ability to influence directions. The then HR director was chair of the group and was influential in moving the work forward.

At the same time I continued with the original 'healthy workplace' sessions with interested teams and leaders. We started to get a few activities going again that had been present, but there wasn't any strategic integration into the business. It was great that a large piece of work was around new organisational values and behaviours, as this aligned well with the work.

Our steering group developed a strategy based on the WHO healthy workplace model. Probably a bit ambitious for the beginning of the journey, but it was a start and we did achieve some of the original aims. Our HR director decided to move on and we were in abeyance for a while until a new one started. We were fortunate that they were very supportive and instrumental in moving the work forward. Opportunely the healthcare evidence that links staff health and wellbeing to safety, quality of experience, care and outcomes was growing. Additionally, discussions and the evidence regarding wellbeing were expanding rapidly. Dr Pat Alley, who was part of our group, was quoted as saying that if the Health Boards demonstrated 'the same sort of care to their health workforce as they expected the health workforce to demonstrate to their patients, that would be a great message'.

Healthy workplaces now

Where are we now and what are we doing? The Healthy Workplaces Steering Group continues to lead the work using the WHO healthy workplace definition and action model as our basis and aligning with Te Whare Tapa Whā.

> *What and when:* Healthy Workplaces, a three-year strategy (Sept. 2016–2019) with an annual review. In this we discuss the drivers; the benefits right from a ground level perspective up to the NZ economy; what are the enablers and alignments; what is the supporting evidence base; what are the opportunities; and how we were going to build a healthy workplace, with a conclusion and call for action.
>
> *Why:* What are some of our drivers? We have an ageing workforce and population; increasing long-term conditions that affect our staff and population and the sustainability of healthcare itself; financial and economic constraints; a predicted shortfall internationally of health professionals; we are rapidly growing; increasing workloads, constant change and well-documented evidence of increasing stress, fatigue, burnout, low morale and job satisfaction levels in healthcare. The evidence of the inextricable links between staff health and wellbeing and the safety, quality of experience, care and outcomes for patients/clients and their families/whanau is overwhelming.
>
> In addition we have new health and safety legislation, the Health and Safety at Work Act (2015). There is more of a risk management approach, where it is not only the physical but also the psychosocial risks that need to be managed.
>
> *How:* The organisation already undertakes a wide variety of actions to support staff health, safety and wellbeing, and for this strategy we wanted to focus on activities the literature described as benefits but where we didn't have current work in progress. The method we used to identify these activities was an environment scan (PESTLE) and a SWOT. These methods helped us

identify factors of success/opportunity and whether we had an action which matched that factor. We then focused on putting in place actions where we had a partial or no match to the relevant success factor or opportunity. We also used information from a health and wellbeing survey of over 650 staff that identified what areas they would be interested in.

An overview of the strategy was presented in two models (PESTLE and SWOT):

Strategic framework:

Systems and value: Aspiring to create healthy workplaces through a strategic quality improvement model with the principles of 'good work' will contribute to the organisational priorities, purpose, values, national health priorities and the Treaty of Waitanagi. Use a collective leadership approach with flexibility and adaptability to look at systems through focusing on engagement, diversity, empowerment of ownership of personal health and wellbeing, as well as supporting the psychosocial, psychological and physical wellbeing and safety of all staff.

Strategic drivers: As noted in the 'why' section, these were distributed using the WHO descriptors: creating healthy workplaces is the right, legal and smart thing to do.

Evidence based: Our strategy is built around the evidence whilst creating our own evidence.

Outcomes: Focused on three levels, those of enhancement of: staff health and wellbeing; patient/client quality of care, experience and outcomes; and impacts on the business, sustainability of healthcare, societal health and wellbeing, all contributing to the NZ economy.

Outcomes model:

Meet our organisational priorities – better patient experience and outcomes:
Supporting the patient experience program through staff and patient feedback systems.
Undertaking a stock-take of our diversity actions, to identify ways of better supporting inclusivity and equity in the workplace.

Promote improved staff experience, engagement and feedback:
Through a staff survey; representation on the governance Health, Safety and Wellbeing committee; support for existing workload management and actions; fostering effective teamwork and workplace culture; development of communication framework and empowering local teams to establish their own healthy workplace activities.

Our people report that their health, safety and wellbeing are supported in the workplace, and staff wellbeing, unplanned absence and turnover improve:
This area looked at age-friendly environments; retirement and financial planning; health and wellbeing expos; walking challenging; wellbeing and mindfulness sessions; lifestyle checks; completing gym builds; work organisation; safe design; fatigue and shift work and a focus on our top three incident types.

An evidence base that supports the healthy workplaces strategy:

Undertaking a stock-take of healthy workplace activities to start connecting the dots and acknowledging the work we are doing. Development of own benchmark and measures, online resources, exploring the Health Promoting Hospitals framework and building on existing networking with experts and supporting related research.

Enablers and alignments: Commitment by the senior management team to support the work. The work aligns with organisational strategic directions, purpose, promise and values and is collaborative work with the main union partners. In addition it aligns with key government priorities and directions.

Opportunities: To lead the way, walk the talk.

What are the benefits of providing healthy workplaces in healthcare?

Individual: Improved personal health and wellbeing; resilience and increased engagement with being valued, respected and higher job satisfaction, morale, trust, meaning and purpose.

Team: Increased cohesion and effectiveness of teams, leading to better outcomes; creating supportive learning and valued environments, which increases productivity whilst fostering collaboration, creativity and innovation.

Organisational: Increases: quality of safety of care, outcomes and experiences for patients/clients; productivity; engagement; collaborative work; trust; staff health and wellbeing; industrial relations; creativity and innovation; attraction of a quality workforce and contribution to the Ministry of Health high-level outcomes and the reputation of organisation. Decreases: sickness/absence; presenteeism; recruitment and retention costs; incidents involving patients and staff.

Patient/client, family/whanau: Improved quality and safety of service, care, outcomes and experience; fewer incidents and more meaningful interactions with an engaged workforce.

Community and society: Contribution to improving the health and wellbeing of society and influencing the social determinants of health and increases trust in the healthcare system.

Economy: Contributes to affordable, sustainable, safer healthcare provision and overall a productive society.

Internationally there is a call for action to develop healthy workplaces for the future success of a safe, sustainable, effective healthcare service. It is recognised that healthcare workers are struggling to provide quality care, and there are profound impacts on the quality, effectiveness and efficiency of patient/client outcomes and experience through the health and wellbeing of the workforce. I like Simon Stevens' quote from the NHS in the UK: 'creating healthy, supportive workplaces is no longer a nice to have, it's a must do'.

We are only at the beginning of our journey, so I am sure that there will be much to learn along the way. We will need that collective leadership approach and to be adaptable and flexible to achieve success. I was heartened to hear our HR director say that a national group has a work stream regarding healthy workplaces and agreed to use the WHO definition and action model as a guide. Additionally they will use some of our work, and I feel that this is a testament to the fact we are on the right track.

NZ now: So where is NZ now? Dame Carol Black always said it would be like the ripple effect. Well, maybe finally the ripples are beginning to get a bit closer! There is growing interest in the whole field, with government agencies such as the Health Promotion Agency and public health organisations providing information and programs on how to improve health and wellbeing in workplaces. An existing Consensus Statement on the Health Benefits of Work is being reviewed with a focus on 'good work'. In addition there are a number of leading workplaces that are doing some amazing work and various conferences now that are incorporating this field. But are we connecting the dots or is there still silo working and thinking?

NZ does have a new Health Strategy; it does allude to the workplace diagrammatically, but there is little in there to show how they might include workplaces in improving the health and wellbeing of all New Zealanders. The new Health and Safety at Work Act (2015) may influence directions with the risk management approach, but how much focus is there on the psychosocial risks? The Healthy Work Strategy from WorkSafe NZ will start to bring the importance of health back into health and safety, and wellbeing is mentioned. In NZ we need more cross-government approaches, some funding and to walk the talk. We need to share our stories, our successes and challenges. We need business cases to guide and get buy-in. I get very envious as I see the international work, support and funding.

Future directions: I believe that health, safety, wellbeing and work are inextricably linked and wonder why we separate them? Psychosocial risks are the greatest health and safety challenge of the modern-day workplace and they significantly impact wellbeing. We need to understand them and start to manage them as any other risk. We have to stop the silo working and work collaboratively, with a collective leadership approach. We need policy that is evidence-informed to lead practice, but practice needs to guide policy to make it real. I believe that to move forward we need to look holistically and strategically, using a quality improvement methodology with some common language and understanding to influence a culture and behaviour change.

If we look at definitions of 'good work, healthy work, meaningful work', most of the components are to do with the psychosocial environment. Can we have these without healthy workplaces? So does wellbeing come before engagement or does engagement come through increasing the focus on wellbeing or does it matter?

There are numerous definitions of wellbeing. From the mental health world, we have the five winning ways of wellbeing: give, connect, keep learning, take notice and be active. Gallup identify a need to focus on five essential elements for wellbeing, those of career, social, financial, physical and community (Gallup, 2012). If we embed these principles, they will add benefit to workplaces and society. There is so much information out there now on what makes a good day at work. My own research and ongoing work identify that core to healthy workplaces are: being valued, supported and communicated with and with good leadership, teamwork and job factors. So how many of these are set by wellbeing programs? How many cost money? Or is it about that essence of going back to basics and treating others as we would like to be treated?

Workplaces are a microcosm of society and play a pivotal role in improving wellbeing at multiple levels. It is imperative that we take responsibility and action for the influences and impacts we have.

We can create healthy workplaces which contribute to improving wellbeing and there are some very crucial elements:

> Leadership: Engaging, collaborative, collective, authentic, values based, compassionate, supportive, visible leadership is essential. The wellbeing of the people at the heart of the business is absolutely critical as this builds trust and engagement. We need to build managers' competencies but a focus on front-line managers is crucial. This enables and empowers them to have a greater understanding of the impact on the health and wellbeing of their staff, but also their outcomes.
> Engagement: Focusing on multiple ways of increasing employee engagement will improve wellbeing as this will contribute to building trust and meaning and purpose for the people, which is vital to an organisation's performance. This increases collaborative work and discretionary effort.
> Teamwork: A focus on effective teamwork is essential for increasing individual, team and organisational wellbeing and resilience, performance and success.
> Measures: Most businesses require some sorts of measures, so work out what is most useful.

Me personally: It has been an incredible journey for me personally, and still is, as I am being asked to speak in all sorts of places in and out of healthcare. I am very privileged to have the support of many people internationally and in NZ who believe in what I am saying; they often give me the strength to carry on when the going gets tough. I would like to thank my own organisation for their support of the work.

If I am asked, has the work I am doing made a difference? Well, on reflection I think I am beginning to see changes in many places. Could I measure them? No, not at this stage, but the stories that I hear from ground level keep me going and grounded. We have a society that focuses on 'what's in it for me', and to influence change and behaviour we have to move beyond this. I am still being asked to do the 'healthy workplace' sessions in workplaces, and I wouldn't change those original themes. If we develop healthy workplaces, we can build individual, team and organisational wellbeing and resilience. It is good to empower individuals to improve their resilience, but we must not forget the critical role of the environment they work in.

What would I do if I were to start again?

Yes, I would use the WHO healthy workplace definition and action model. It links health, safety and wellbeing and incorporates psychosocial risks and gives a framework of what to work off. I would also use Te Whare Tapa Whā, as it makes health and wellbeing real to the people. I would get leadership commitment and a steering group of interested people. I would do a stock-take of what we are already doing, acknowledge the good work and identify the gaps, as well as engaging with the workers as to what they are interested in in order to work out a plan. Don't forget the basics though, as a focus on leadership styles, engagement, teamwork and measures are crucial for success. Use the evidence; I get really excited as I see more and more being released. Have I got it all right or all the answers? Absolutely not; you need to find what way works in your organisation and then be flexible and adaptable. I look forward to the future with the challenges and the opportunities. Two quotes that I really relate to are:

> If you keep on doing the same things and expect things to change, then that's a definition of insanity.
>
> *Einstein*

> One person can make a difference, and everyone should try.
>
> *J. F. Kennedy*

As the WHO identifies, creating healthy workplaces 'is the right, legal and smart thing to do and contributes to wellbeing at multiple levels'.

Refrences

Cooper, R., Boyko, C. and Codinhoto, R. (2008) 'Mental Capital and Wellbeing: Making the Most of Ourselves', *Foresight*, pp. 1–22.

Durie, M. (1994) *Whaiora: Māori Health Development*. Auckland: Oxford University Press, p. 70.

Kouzes, J. M. and Posner, B. Z. (2007) *The Leadership Challenge*, 4th edn. San Francisco, CA: John Wiley & Sons Inc., p. 26.

Rath, T. and Hartner, J. (2012) *The Five Essential Elements of Wellbeing*. Available at: http://businessjournal.gallup.com/content/126884/five-essential-elements-wellbing.aspx.

Stevens, S. (2015) 'Simon Stevens Announces Major Drive to Improve Health in NHS Workplace'. NHS England. Available at: www.england.nhs.uk/2015/09/nhs-workplace/

Television New Zealand (3 November 2011). *Health Professionals under the Spotlight*.

World Health Organization (2010) *Healthy Workplaces: A Model for Action*. Available at: http://apps.who.int/iris/bitstream/10665/44307/1/9789241599313_eng.pdf

Dr Justin Varney

National Lead for Adult Health and Wellbeing, Public Health England

Achieving legendary workplace health and wellbeing

For too many managers there seems to be a fundamental disconnection with the issue of workplace health and wellbeing and why it is important for businesses and line managers. If you get it, then the connections are clear and often you are one of the evangelical, slightly maverick and out-on-a-limb members of the team. If you don't, then staff health and wellbeing sits as a concept in an abstract and slightly mystic hippy space somewhere between the legends of the pleasure dome of Kubla Khan and the Elven woods of Middle Earth, not quite health and safety and not quite organisational development or HR.

For converts it seems obvious that a healthy workplace is essential to a healthy life. In England over two thirds of adults are in employment and they spend on average over a third of their waking hours over the week in the workplace. So investing in health has to happen during the working day or otherwise a third of the potential time for change and investment is wasted. It's no different from the focus on schools as key spaces for investing and shaping children's behaviours – why would it be any different for adults who are in many ways equally institutionalised in workplaces?

The second seemingly obvious connection is that if you want to have a successful business, then you need your staff to be present, healthy and happy. More and more the research is telling us that the bottom line is affected by more than physical absenteeism. Getting the most from your colleagues is about ensuring they are present both physically and mentally, and about reducing presenteeism and absenteeism. Successful teams and businesses support their staff to invest in their health, be connected, empowered and engaged with their work to produce high quality products or customer experiences.

Too often we seem to compartmentalise investing in our own, and our colleagues', health and wellbeing into a separate space from work, creating cultures where, if it is considered at all, it is in the 'nice to do' rather than the 'core business' bit of the conversation. The evidence would say this is a bad choice and that businesses that don't invest in their staff have higher staff turnover and higher sickness absence costs, lose productivity and face reputation and outcome risks due to staff errors.

Sadly it often takes a catastrophic loss of a key member of staff through a health event to change attitudes. Tragically for some businesses it has taken suicide to get the board and senior management team to shift their paradigm of workplace health, although I have also seen deaths through suicide in organisations that have spectacular investment and leadership for staff health and wellbeing, reminding us all that workplaces, like schools, are only ever going to be a (significant) part of the support for an individual's health and wellbeing.

We often find ourselves, and our colleagues, trying to force all the 'healthy stuff' into the weekends and evenings where it feels like it is competing with relationship time and the daily chores of everyday life such as paying bills and fixing the cable TV. In reality many of these other time allocations can be health improving, but more of that later. As you move into a management role, it is easier and easier to compartmentalise your life and those of the people you work with, especially as diaries become more and more challenging and the persistent background ping of email becomes the drum beat of the workplace treadmill, although this happens to more and more of us now much earlier in our careers.

As you rise up through the management layers and move from being a delivery agent to a strategic leader, it can be easy to forget some of the practical barriers and realities of life on the 'shop floor' and lose yourself in your diary. One of the best leadership tips I ever got from my father, later reinforced by Cathy Watkins, Chief Executive of Newham General Hospital, where I did my first junior doctor job, was to regularly walk the floor and talk to people. Spending time with colleagues who are in different parts of the business helps you as a senior manager to understand some of the details of delivery and to meet the people who know that cog of the system best. Whether in the post room or the customer-facing shop floor, there are colleagues who have real nuggets of wisdom and insight. Walking the floor shouldn't be a 'state visit' type moment and in some organisations it can take a while to nest in as an approach, but it is totally worth it. Having tried to practise it throughout my career, I can vouch for it as a really important way to reconnect with colleagues and get a lot of soft intelligence about the wellbeing of the workforce.

High performing businesses recognise that engaging staff and co-producing approaches to staff health and wellbeing are key to making them work. If colleagues are connected to the strategy and delivery plan, then they are more likely to participate both in the activities and in the evaluation and feedback loop.

When I first joined Public Health England, I was tasked with developing a workplace health and wellbeing strategy (2014–2016) which was rooted in the evidence but built with staff involvement and delivered a framework that could work across over 150 sites to about 5600 staff who had joined the organisation from over 160 different organisations.

We started with pulling together the evidence. It's probably important to share that this was a small part of my responsibilities; my primary job was leading a programme of work to improve adult health and wellbeing in England. This was an adjunct to help connect policy and practice during a period of transition and I had one member of staff working on the delivery programme as well as developing the strategy.

There is a range of NICE guidance with recommendations for evidence-based interventions in the workplace, and we also drew on the road map for this evidence that local workplace health and wellbeing accreditation schemes such as the Liverpool Workplace Wellbeing Charter and North East Better Work Award provided. Organisationally there was a clear commitment to try to work towards the Marmot definition of 'good work' across the business; this was driven by reputation as well as a cultural commitment from the top down that we should be working towards being an exemplar organisation.

Features of good work

1. Free of core features of precariousness, such as lack of stability and high risk of job loss, lack of safety measures (exposure to toxic substances, elevated risks of accidents, and the absence of minimal standards of employment protection).
2. Enables the working person to exert some control through participatory decision-making on matters such as the place and the timing of work and the tasks to be accomplished.
3. Places appropriately high demands on the working person, both in terms of quantity and quality, without overtaxing their resources and capabilities and without doing harm to their physical and mental health.
4. Provides fair employment in terms of earnings reflecting productivity and in terms of employers' commitment towards guaranteeing job security.
5. Offers opportunities for skills training, learning and promotion prospects within a life course perspective, sustaining health and work ability and stimulating the growth of an individual's capabilities.
6. Prevents social isolation and any form of discrimination and violence.
7. Enables workers to share relevant information within the organisation, to participate in organisational decision-making and collective bargaining and to guarantee procedural justice in case of conflicts.
8. Aims at reconciling work and extra-work/family demands in ways that reduce the cumulative burden of multiple social roles.
9. Attempts to reintegrate sick and disabled people into full employment wherever possible.
10. Contributes to workers' wellbeing by meeting the basic psychological needs of self-efficacy, self-esteem, sense of belonging and meaningfulness.

The Marmot Review Team. *Fair Society, Healthy Lives: Strategic Review of Health Inequalities in England Post-2010*. London: Marmot Review Team, 2010.

At that stage we had very little evidence about what the organisation needed; there was existing data on sickness absence and some general data on engagement and wellbeing from the civil service people survey but nothing specific on health risk behaviour or issues. So we commissioned a survey of employee health and wellbeing through our employee assistance provider. The questions were developed with input from colleagues across the organisation, trying to choose questions which could be benchmarked against national data – as this was a first for the organisation there was no local trend data to judge the level of need. Some 21% of the organisation participated in the survey and the sample was representative of the wider organisational demographic and geographical distribution. The survey highlighted that although we had some good news – perhaps unsurprisingly for a health agency we had much lower levels of smoking than in the general population – there were significant challenges around mental health, particularly stress, and inactivity. The findings from the survey were presented to the senior management team and published on the intranet for all colleagues to access. They were combined with the research evidence and we developed a draft strategy which focused on three key outcome measures.

We ran an open consultation with colleagues which focused on five key questions:

Are the guiding principles of the strategy the right ones?

Do the specific areas for action reflect the perceptions of the staff wellbeing needs?

Do the cross-cutting actions reflect the right emphasis and approach needed to implement the strategy?

Are there other ways you feel we can monitor the effectiveness of the strategy moving forward?

What areas for action in 14/15 and 15/16 would you like to see emphasised for PHE staff wellbeing?

Lots of staff engaged with the consultation and we also ran specific engagement events across the estate to enable and encourage participation from as broad a geographical footprint as possible. The consultation provided some really helpful feedback and highlighted some opportunities and synergies we hadn't identified from the central head office way of thinking.

PHE Health and Wellbeing Strategy 2014–16 Core Principles

Providing strong foundations

- Through preventing and mitigating workplace risk in our health and safety and facilities approach
- Proactively supporting and protecting staff through our occupational health function
- Ensuring that the organisation has the policy and protocol framework that supports staff
- A mandatory training programme which gives all staff a common set of skills and understanding to work in a diverse and multi-professional organisation

Supporting development and engagement

- Through regular appraisal and regular supervision with trained and supported line managers
- Ongoing two-way communication and engagement with staff through face to face events and engagement as well as virtual communication

- Ongoing dialogue and partnership with trade unions and professional bodies
- Training and development opportunities which reflect the breadth of the multi-professional workforce across PHE

Branching opportunities for growth and maximising potential

- Through providing an environment and organisational culture that supports healthy choices and lifestyles
- Intervention programmes to promote opportunities for individuals to develop and enhance their own physical and mental health and wellbeing, drawing on PHE's external ambitions and campaigns

The final strategy used a tree analogy to set out three core principles of: providing strong foundations, supporting development and engagement through the trunk and providing branching opportunities for growth and maximising potential. There were three key outcome measures:

- Close the gap in the self-reported wellbeing indicators for our staff and those of the general population by 2017.
- Close the gap for the average number of sickness absence days per employee between PHE and the UK average.
- Close the gap for adults achieving an average of 150 minutes of physical activity a week between our staff and the national average.

The strategy was approved and ratified by the PHE National Executive and supported in its implementation through a network of 160 trained volunteer workplace health and wellbeing champions and a programme of health and wellbeing initiatives embedded through internal communications support and local activation by the champions.

In 2016/17 I stepped back from leading the internal staff health and wellbeing programme and it was reintegrated in our in-house occupational health service. Since the strategy was launched, there has been consistent improvement in sickness absence rates and HR have led a significant programme of work with line managers to improve sickness absence management. Despite massive organisational change and restricting self-reporting, wellbeing indicators have held steady, which we consider a significant success and a reflection of much of the work delivered through the programme.

Perhaps our most visible impact has been on physical activity, where we are in the third year of our corporate physical activity challenge, in partnership for the last two years with the County Sport Partnership Network. About 20% of the organisation is actively participating in the challenge and across the estate we have seen staff self-mobilising to lead active lunch-break walks and good uptake of the Cycle2Work scheme. The shift in the organisational approach to physical activity has also penetrated our event organisation, so that at all major PHE events we offer physical activity taster sessions such as lunchtime walks, often in partnership with the Ramblers, and active travel plans and standing 'poser tables' are the norm. The chief executive has even made a public pledge to staff to use the stairs rather than the lift to his fifth floor office, and committed to pay a personal fine if he is ever caught in the lift!

It is clear from my direct experience, and from the businesses that I have worked in and with over the years, that it is possible to develop a coherent approach to workplace health and wellbeing that is co-produced with colleagues and built on the evidence base to be effective and impactful. Delivering effective support for workplace health and wellbeing is fundamental, and cost-effective, for a productive and agile business. Achieving perfect workplace health and wellbeing may well be a fantasy in today's rapidly changing climate, and what is 'perfect' for one business may not work at all in another, as the emerging evidence base shows. However, like all good legends, perhaps the most important part is the journey rather than the destination . . .

Tony Vickers-Byrne

Director of HR, Public Health England

I've always had a need for heroes

I grew up in Wythenshawe, Manchester, in the 1960s, with a dysfunctional television but a voracious appetite for sport and adventure stories. My three favourite places were Old Trafford football and cricket grounds and the mobile library which drove around the housing estate. A new purpose built library opened in 1971 at the Wythenshawe Forum, host of the 1976 World Snooker Final between the dominant player of the 1970s, Ray Reardon, and the 25-year-old Alex Higgins, of whom more later. I devoured stories of ancient and medieval heroes: Jason and the Argonauts, Roland and Oliver, the heroes of early French legend, Horatio holding the bridge in Rome . . .

My sporting heroes were Best, Law and Charlton, the heart of Matt Busby's second great Manchester United team. I remember Bobby Charlton showing his emotion after the World Cup Final in 1966, the European Cup in 1968 and also when he appeared on *This is Your Life* and was reminded about his friends and teammates who died in the Munich Air Crash in 1958. When I visit Old Trafford today, I always spend some time at the memorial plaque on the East Stand beside the Munich clock showing the date of 6 February 1958.

Across Trafford Park, Clive Lloyd, future captain of the West Indies all conquering cricket team, was the great figure, both languid and destructive in the same movement, and Lancashire's first black cricket captain. When Clive played for the West Indies, they were my team, even against England. The first inklings of my interest in diversity were stirred by Clive and his calm authoritative leadership.

As the television became more reliable, with transistors replacing valves, supplemented by regular trips to the Tatton Cinema in Gatley, my heroes became more diverse: Peter O'Toole in *Lawrence of Arabia*; Omar Sharif in *Dr Zhivago*; Frank Sinatra in the *Devil at 4 O'Clock*, saving the children while the Pacific Island explodes. All of them flawed, outsiders, their own men, all of them dying at the end.

In the early 1980s at university, Alex Higgins emerged as a hero again. Exam revision went on hold as we watched him, vulnerable, exciting and unpredictable, in the World Snooker Final in 1982, collapsing in tears as he hugged his young baby and wife. His flaws and the stories in the tabloid press were forgotten in the human emotion of the evening.

As I left university and joined the NHS, more by luck than judgement, my heroes were still on the sporting field and screen. My main motivation at the time was to move quickly up the career ladder, changing roles every few months to achieve promotion across the London NHS. I didn't feel a deep relationship with my personnel and clinical colleagues in the hospitals – at the time I had a reputation for getting things done and taking the tough decisions, often affecting people's careers. The objective was my key driver.

Looking back, I was raw and inexperienced and being appointed as an HR director at the age of 31 was a mistake for me and the NHS.

I finally began to mature due to my first real hero at work. But of course there is a sporting connection. In 2003, Gareth Goodier joined the Royal Brompton and Harefield NHS Trust in London from Australia. Gareth was a doctor, born and trained in England, who had made the transition to becoming a successful healthcare chief executive in Australia. Under Gareth, we set out to transform the culture at the two hospitals, where some of the world's most eminent heart and lung physicians and surgeons worked to save the lives of desperately ill patients of all ages from across the world.

Gareth was a transformational, charismatic figure in the Trust, bringing in anti-bullying and harassment training programmes, introducing action learning sets, values and behaviours and talent management programmes. He was visible across all the wards and departments, positioning the staff as the 'heart and lungs' of the hospitals.

In early 2004, less than a year after he had joined, Gareth's wife was diagnosed with terminal cancer. As I write this, I still feel the shock of when he told me the news. Gareth continued to be totally committed over the coming months as he led a complex organisation, facing major organisational change, with dignity and courage. Gareth always said that the kindness and support of the Trust chair, Lord Tony Newton, helped him through, enabling him to balance his care for his wife with the care for his staff.

As the cancer progressed, Gareth moved to Brisbane to be with his wife and her family in the last few weeks and to record the sunsets off the Gold Coast in Queensland. He was still leading the Trust back in England via email and phone.

In early August 2004, I received an email from Gareth saying that his wife had died earlier that morning surrounded by her family. Her last sunset had been exceptionally beautiful. Gareth went on to tell me where to collect the tickets that he had bought previously to watch Manchester United and Chelsea play at Stamford Bridge the following day, as he knew that Tom, my 7-year-old United fanatic, would love to see them play.

I would have done anything for Gareth.

I am privileged to work for Public Health England, led by Duncan Selbie, a chief executive who puts people before systems. PHE works to protect and improve the nation's health and tackle inequalities. A key part of my work is to encourage all employers to invest in the health and wellbeing of their staff and, over the course of the last few years, hardly a day has gone past without me discovering another initiative, either in a major multinational or in an SME employing a few dozen staff, where leaders are putting the welfare and development of their colleagues before their own – for the benefit of the customer or patient. I've helped support the work of Dame Carol Black, Justin Varney, the author of a case study in this book, Kevin Fenton, our Director of Health and Wellbeing, Cary Cooper and countless other courageous and forward thinking people whose business is the health and wellbeing of others. I am able to learn about selfless and compassionate initiatives across all parts of the UK employment sector; a key part of PHE's role is to spread the word about best practice and also the mistakes that organisations have made on the way to improving their service.

I am always surprised at how humble the great leaders are. I realise the arrogance of my early years as a leader and the conflicts that I could have avoided with more self-awareness at the time.

Perhaps the most defining day of my working life took place in April 2013, when I was introduced to Aidan Halligan. Much has been written about Aidan, a doctor from a wealthy area of Dublin who devoted his life to supporting the disadvantaged and vulnerable people across society.

Aidan set up Pathway, a homeless charity in East London, when he was moved by the plight of the people he met living on the streets. Aidan was director of Well North, a Public Health England initiative to improve the health of the underprivileged in Manchester and other parts of the north of England. He also set up the NHS Staff College, developed with a strong emphasis on the skills and experiences that NHS leaders could learn from the military. Aidan visited Camp Bastion in Afghanistan, a truly multinational A and E, where he saw real team work, regardless of rank, operating in conditions and saving lives in working conditions that few could imagine.

> At its core, leadership is a purely moral and emotional activity. It is unconnected with seniority and only loosely related to intellect and it is about the ability to engage, motivate and improve. It is delivered by our values and implies having moral courage, integrity and the conviction to accept accountability.

Aidan died unexpectedly in his sleep on 27 April 2015 at the age of 57.

When I heard the news, I felt the same sense of disbelief I did when Princess Diana died in 1997, when I had turned the car around on a Sunday morning and forgot about going to the gym. Over the course of the next few weeks there were visible outpourings of grief from the colleagues that Aidan had devoted his working life to – the homeless, ex-prisoners, drug users and other vulnerable groups. Newspaper articles and social media articles appeared telling personal stories of the courage and compassion that Aidan displayed every day. At Warren Street underground station, opposite University College London Hospital where the NHS Staff College was based, an unknown person had written on the whiteboard in the foyer:

> RIP Aidan Halligan – Leadership is doing the right thing on a difficult day.

One of Aidan's favourite quotes.

Aidan's legacy is being kept alive by the work of Pathway and the newly formed Staff College, by the work of the role models he helped develop in disadvantaged communities and by his impact on leaders across healthcare settings.

Over the course of 2015, I was introduced to a number of life affirming and life changing initiatives through my work with PHE. Lord Kamlesh Patel of Bradford introduced me to Project SEARCH, a work experience programme developed in

University of Cincinnati Hospital for young adults with learning disabilities, providing real work in different locations with the support of local authorities, schools, charitable foundations and, most importantly, committed managers and staff across the host organisation. After the graduation ceremony in Bradford Hospital for the Project SEARCH students, I committed to Kamlesh that I would raise awareness of the power and importance of Project SEARCH whenever I met new people on an individual or group basis. There have been a number of raised eyebrows when I have regularly diverted discussions at meetings to tell my experiences of Project SEARCH in action and the transformation it has made in the young adults, their families and friends, and the managers and staff in the host organisation. Over 65% of the students obtain paid work after completing the programme, compared to 6% of adults with learning disabilities across the UK. Quite simply, introducing Project SEARCH at our Colindale laboratories in north-west London and spreading the message about its importance to my networks are the most important things I have ever done in my working life.

Aidan's example and work, initiatives like Project SEARCH, the work of charities supporting ex-military staff who are wounded, ill or sick to gain work experience, and Mosaic Clubhouse, providing work opportunities for adults with mental health conditions, have inspired me to take 'action'.

In late 2016, following advice from Justin Varney, I set up a fledgling compassionate management social movement. In the early days I occasionally questioned what I was doing – in my mind only – as some people I worked with thought I was going through a second, older, mid-life crisis. Compassion has not been a word readily associated with me during my career. I was known as somebody who was called in to do the tough stuff.

Over the course of the last year I have been supported by Duncan, my chief executive – himself a mentee of Aidan – during a period of turbulence and ill health in my blended family. At the same time there have been ongoing significant organisational changes and staffing reductions, but we have been able to increase the levels of staff engagement across PHE.

I am continuing to discover new stories and examples of how managers and staff across all parts of the UK are putting the welfare and development of their colleagues, customers and patients before their own, working in partnership with other passionate and expert people. I am able to communicate these across the growing social movement – that's all I do.

I have been surprised about how many people have joined the 'social movement' – a phrase I would not have associated with myself – over the last few months and we are planning our first conferences and campaigns at the time of writing. Cary's endorsement for the movement at an early stage was invaluable.

Doubtless, in the months and years to come, more experienced campaigners and social media experts will take forward the importance of compassion and action in the workplace on a wider stage. In the short time I have been involved I have noticed a narrowing of the gap between the leadership styles of successful public and private sector organisations.

I am happy to have taken forward a part of Aidan's legacy and also to have developed myself at the same time as a leader for my incredibly committed and expert

HR team and also as a husband, father and friend. Although I have regular lapses, I am now more aware when I'm having them.

The last word to my hero Aidan:

> Leadership is going into the unknown with courage – people respect courage and they respect compassion.

REFERENCES

(All website URLs were accessed on 6 June 2017.)

Age in the Workplace (2016) London. Available at: http://age.bitc.org.uk.

Bakker, A. and Demerouti, E. (2008) 'Towards a Model of Work Engagement', *Career Development International*, 13(3), pp. 209–223.

Balogun, J. and Hope-Hailey, V. (2008) *Exploring Strategic Change*, 3rd edn. Harlow: Prentice Hall.

Barslund, M. (2015) 'Extending Working Lives: The Case of Denmark'. Available: CEPS.

Bateman, T. and Organ, D. (1983) 'Job Satisfaction and the Good Soldier: The Relationship between Affect and Employee "Citizenship"', *Academy of Management Journal (pre-1986)*, 26(4), p. 587.

BBC (2017) 'Simon Wessely on Unexplained Medical Syndromes'. In: Wessely, S. (ed.) *The Life Scientific*. London: BBC.

Black, C. (2015) *Workplace Wellbeing Charter*. London: Public Health England.

Black, C., Frost, D. and Department of Work and Pensions (2011) *Health at Work: An Independent Review of Sickness Absence*. London: HM Government.

Bradford, B., Quinton, P., Myhill, A. and Porter, G. (2014) 'Why Do "the Law" Comply? Procedural Justice, Group Identification and Officer Motivation in Police Organizations', *European Journal of Criminology*, 11(1), pp. 110–131.

Bruce, J. (2013) *The Cost of Stress in Your Organization and What You Should Do About It*. Available at: www.mequilibrium.com/wp-content/uploads/2013/03/3-1-13-FINAL.pdf.

Burton, J. (2010) *World Health Organization Healthy Workplace Framework and Model*. Geneva: WHO. Available at: www.who.int/occupational_health/healthy_workplace_framework.pdf.

Cannon, W. (1915) *Bodily Changes in Pain, Hunger, Fear, and Rage*. New York: D. Appleton & Co.

Casey, G. W. (2014) 'Leading in a VUCA World', *Fortune*, 169(5), p. 75.

Chaskalson, M. (2014) *Mindfulness in Eight Weeks: The Revolutionary 8 Week Plan to Clear Your Mind and Calm Your Life*. London: Harper.

CIPD (2014) *Managing an Age-Diverse Workforce: Employer and Employee Views*. Available at: www.cipd.co.uk/hr-resources/managing-age-diverse-workforce-infographic.aspx.

CIPD (2015) *Absence Management Report 2015*, CIPD Simply Health. Available at: www. cipd.co.uk/hr-resources/survey-reports/absence-management-2015.aspx.

CIPD (2017) 'One Million More Older People Need to Be in Work by 2022'. Available: CIPD.

Collinson, D. (2012) 'Prozac Leadership and the Limits of Positive Thinking', *Leadership*, 8(2), pp. 87–107.

Cooper, C. L. (2004) *Stress: A Brief History*. Malden, MA: Blackwell.

Cooper, C. L. and Cartwright, S. (1997) 'An Intervention Strategy for Workplace Stress', *Journal of Psychosomatic Research*, 43(1), pp. 7–16.

Cornum, R. (2012) *Can We Teach Resilience?* Available from The Young Foundation.

Crawford, E. R., Lepine, J. A. and Rich, B. L. (2010) 'Linking Job Demands and Resources to Employee Engagement and Burnout: A Theoretical Extension and Meta-Analytic Test', *Journal of Applied Psychology*, 95(5), pp. 834–848.

Davies, S. (2016) *Britain's Healthiest Workplace Report, 2016*. RAND Europe. Available at: www.vitality.co.uk/business/healthiest-workplace/findings/.

Deal, T. and Kennedy, A. (1982) *Organization Cultures: The Rites and Rituals of Organization Life*. Reading: Addison Wesley.

Diener, E. (2000) 'Subjective Well-Being: The Science of Happiness and a Proposal for a National Index', *American Psychologist*, 55(1), p. 34.

Diener, E. and Biswas-Diener, R. (2008) *Happiness: Unlocking the Mysteries of Psychological Wealth*. Oxford: Wiley-Blackwell.

Gayton, S. D. and Lovell, G. P. (2012) 'Resilience in Ambulance Service Paramedics and Its Relationships with Well-Being and General Health', *Traumatology*, 18(1), pp. 58–64.

Gerich, J. (2015) 'Leaveism and Illness-Related Behaviour', *Occupational Medicine*, 65(9), pp. 746–752.

Government Office for Science (2016) *Future of Ageing: Seminar on Older Workers*. Cowley, London: Gov.uk.

Grant, L. and Kinman, G. (2013) 'Bouncing Back? Personal Representations of Resilience of Student and Experienced Social Workers', *Social Work in Action*, 25(5), pp. 349–366.

Haglund, M. E. M., Nestadt, P. S., Cooper, N. S., Southwick, S. M. and Charney, D. S. (2007) 'Psychobiological Mechanisms of Resilience: Relevance to Prevention and Treatment of Stress-Related Psychopathology', *Development and Psychopathology*, 19(3), pp. 889–920.

Centers for Disease Control and Prevention (2016) *Workplace Health Model*. US: US Department of Health.

Hesketh, I. and Cooper, C. (2014) 'Leaveism at Work', *Occupational Medicine*, 64(3), pp. 146–147.

Hesketh, I. and Cooper, C. (2017) 'Measuring the People Fleet: General Analysis, Interventions and Needs', *Strategic HR Review*, 16(1), pp. 17–23.

Hesketh, I., Cooper, C. and Ivy, J. (2014a) 'Leaveism and Public Sector Reform: Will the Practice Continue?', *Journal of Organizational Effectiveness: People and Performance*, 1(2), pp. 205–212.

Hesketh, I., Smith, J. and Ivy, J. (2014b) 'Keeping the Peelian Spirit: Resilience and Spirituality in Policing', *Police Journal: Theory, Practice and Principles*, 87(3), pp. 154–166.

Hesketh, I., Cooper, C. and Ivy, J. (2015a) 'Well-Being, Austerity and Policing: Is It Worth Investing in Resilience Training?', *The Police Journal: Theory, Practice and Principles*, 88(3), pp. 220–230.

Hesketh, I., Cooper, C. and Ivy, J. (2015b) 'Leaveism and Work–Life Integration: The Thinning Blue Line?', *Policing*, 9(2), pp. 183–194.

Hesketh, I., Cooper, C. and Ivy, J. (2016) 'Wellbeing and Engagement in Policing: The Key to Unlocking Discretionary Effort', *Policing*, pp. 1–12.

Hilary, B. (2012) 'Why It Pays to Be Old – and How to Get Old before Your Years: Companies Capitalize on a Lifetime of Knowledge and Experience', *Human Resource Management International Digest*, 20(1), pp. 35–38.

Hofstede, G. H. (1997) *Cultures and Organizations: Software of the Mind*. New York: McGraw-Hill.

Houdmont, J. and Elliott-Davies, M. (2017) *Officer Demand, Capacity and Welfare Survey: Absence Behaviours RO62/2016*. Police Federation of England and Wales. Available at: www.polfed.org/documents/WelfareSurveyABSENCEBEHAVIOURS-SummaryReport-25-01-2017-V.1.pdf.

HSE (2008) *Working Together to Reduce Stress at Work: A Guide for Employees*. Guidance Booklet, Health and Safety Executive. Available at: www.hse.gov.uk/pubns/indg424.pdf.

HSE (2017) *Health and Work Strategy Plan: Work Related Stress*. Available at: www.hse.gov.uk/statistics/.

Jakubauskas, M. and Wright, S. (2012) *Police at Work: The Wave Five Report*. Sydney: University of Sydney Business School.

Johns, G. (2010) 'Presenteeism in the Workplace: A Review and Research Agenda', *Journal of Organizational Behavior*, 31(4), pp. 519–542.

Johnson, G., Scholes, K. and Whittington, R. (2008) *Exploring Corporate Strategy*, 8th edn. London: Pearson Education.

Johnston, R. and Clark, G. (2008) *Service Operations Management*, 3rd edn. London: Pearson Education.

Kabat-Zinn, J. (2013) *Full Catastrophe Living: Using the Wisdom of Your Body and Mind to Face Stress, Pain and Illness*. New York: Bantam Dell.

Kivimäki, M., Vahtera, J., Elovainio, M., Pentti, J. and Virtanen, M. (2003) 'Human Costs of Organizational Downsizing: Comparing Health Trends between Leavers and Stayers', *American Journal of Community Psychology*, 32(1), pp. 57–67.

Kübler-Ross, E. (1969) *On Death and Dying*. London: Routledge.

Lewin, K. (1947) 'Frontiers in Group Dynamics: Concept, Method and Reality in Social Science; Equilibrium and Social Change', *Human Relations*, 1(1), pp. 5–41.

Luthans, F. (2002) 'The Need for and Meaning of Positive Organizational Behavior', *Journal of Organizational Behavior*, 23(6), pp. 695–706.

MacLeod, D. and Clarke, N. (2009) *Engaging for Success: Enhancing Performance through Employee Engagement*. Department for Business Innovation and Skills. Available at: www.bis.gov.uk/files/file52215.pdf.

Mallack, L. (1998) 'Measuring Resilience in Health Care Provider Organizations', *Health Manpower Management*, 24(4), pp. 148–152.

Marmot, M. G. (1999) *Social Determinants of Health*, edited by Michael Marmot and Richard G. Wilkinson. Oxford: OUP.

Masten, A. S. (2014) 'Global Perspectives on Resilience in Children and Youth', *Child Development*, 85(1), pp. 6–20.

Mintzberg, H. (2008) *Strategy Safari: The Complete Guide through the Wilds of Strategic Management*. Harlow: Financial Times, Prentice Hall.

NICE (2017) *Healthy Workplaces: Improving Employee Mental and Physical Health and Wellbeing*. Available at: www.nice.org.uk/guidance/qs147.

Palmer, S. and Cooper, C. L. (2010) *How to Deal with Stress*, 2nd edn. London: Kogan Page.

Paton, D. (2006) 'Critical Incident Stress Risk in Police Officers: Managing Resilience and Vulnerability', *Traumatology*, 12(3), pp. 198–206.

Rathus, S. A. (2012) *Psychology: Concepts and Connections*, 10th edn. Belmont, CA: Wadsworth.

Rayton, B., Dodge, T. and D'Aneleze, G. (2012) *Engage for Success: The Evidence*. London. Available at: http://opus.bath.ac.uk/35611/1/.

Reardon, J. (1998) 'The History and Impact of Worksite Wellness', *Nursing Economic$*, 16(3), p. 117.

Robertson, I. and Cooper, C. (2010) 'Full Engagement: The Integration of Employee Engagement and Psychological Well-Being', *Leadership and Organization Development Journal*, 31(4), pp. 324–336.

Robertson, I. and Cooper, C. (2011) *Well-Being*. New York: Palgrave Macmillan.

Ryan, R. M. and Deci, E. L. (2001) 'On Happiness and Human Potentials: A Review of Research on Hedonic and Eudaimonic Well-Being', *Annual Review of Psychology*, 52, p. 141.

Ryff, C. D. (1989) 'Happiness Is Everything, or Is It? Explorations on the Meaning of Psychological Well-Being', *Journal of Personality and Social Psychology*, 57(6), pp. 1069–1081.

Ryff, C. D. and Keyes, C. L. (1995) 'The Structure of Psychological Well-Being Revisited', *Journal of Personality and Social Psychology*, 69(4), p. 719.

Rynes, S. L., Colbert, A. E. and Brown, K. G. (2002) 'HR Professionals' Beliefs about Effective Human Resource Practices: Correspondence between Research and Practice', *Human Resource Management*, 41(2), pp. 149–174.

Sapolsky, R. M. (2004) *Why Zebras Don't Get Ulcers*, 3rd edn. New York: Melia Distributor.

Schaufeli, W. and Bakker, A. B. (2004) 'Job Demands, Job Resources, and Their Relationship with Burnout and Engagement: A Multi-sample Study', *Journal of Organizational Behavior*, 25, pp. 293–315.

Schaufeli, W., Salanova, B., González-romá, M., Bakker, V., Bakker, A. and Bakker, B. (2002) 'The Measurement of Engagement and Burnout: A Two Sample Confirmatory Factor Analytic Approach', *Journal of Happiness Studies*, 3(1), pp. 71–92.

Schein, E. H. (2010) *Organizational Culture and Leadership*, 4th edn. San Franciso, CA: Jossey-Bass Publishers.

Schein, E. H., with Schein, P. (2017) *Organizational Culture and Leadership*, 5th edn. Hoboken, NJ: John Wiley and Sons, Inc.

Seligman, M. (2003) *Authentic Happiness: Using the New Positive Psychology to Realize Your Potential for Deep Fulfillment*. London: Nicholas Brealey Publishing.

Seligman, M. (2011) *Flourish: A New Understanding of Happiness and Well-Being – and How to Achieve Them*. London: Nicholas Brealey Publishing.

Selye, H. (1984) *The Stress of Life*. New York: McGraw-Hill.

Sisgold, S. (2015) *Whole Body Intelligence: Get Out of Your Head and Into Your Body to Achieve Greater Wisdom, Confidence, and Success*. New York: Rofale.

Smith, J., Charles, G. and Hesketh, I. (2015) 'Developing Understanding of the Spiritual Aspects to Resilience', *International Journal of Public Leadership*, 11(1), pp. 34–45.

Southwick, S. and Charney, D. (2012a) *Resilience: The Science of Mastering Life's Greatest Challenges*. London: Cambridge University Press.

Southwick, S. and Charney, D. (2012b) 'The Science of Resilience: Implications for the Prevention and Treatment of Depression', *Science*, 338(6103), pp. 79–82.

Suadicani, P., Olesen, K., Bonde, J. and Gyntelberg, F. (2014) 'Psychosocial Work Conditions Associated with Sickness Absence among Hospital Employees', *Occupational Medicine*, 64(7), pp. 503–508.

Syed, M. (2015) *Black Box Thinking: Why Most People Never Learn from Their Mistakes – but Some Do*. London: John Murray Publishers.

Taylor, S. E., Klein, L. C., Lewis, B. P., Gruenewald, T. L., Gurung, R. A. R. and Updegraff, J. A. (2000) 'Biobehavioral Responses to Stress in Females: Tend-and-Befriend, Not Fight-or-Flight', *Psychological Review*, 107(3), pp. 411–429.

Thornton, S. (2015) 'We Must "Re-imagine" Policing in the UK', *The Police Foundation's Annual John Harris Memorial Lecture*, London, 20 July 2015. Online: National Police Chiefs' Council.

Timpson, J. (2016) 'Are You Responsible for Your Employees' Health?', *Professional Manager*. Available at: www.managers.org.uk/insights/news/2016/february/debate-are-you-responsible-for-your-employees-health.

Towers Perrin (2003) *Working Today: Understanding What Drives Employee Engagement*. Available at: www.keepem.com/doc_files/Towers_Perrin_Talent_2003(TheFinal).pdf.

Viner, R. (1999) 'Putting Stress in Life: Hans Selye and the Making of Stress Theory', *Social Studies of Science*, 29(3), pp. 391–410.

Waterman, A. S. (1984) *The Psychology of Individualism*. New York and Eastbourne: Praeger.

WEF (2016) *The Future of Jobs: Employment, Skills and Workforce Strategy for the Fourth Industrial Revolution*. Available at: www3.weforum.org/docs/WEF_Future_of_Jobs.pdf.

WEF (2017) *The Moral Dilemmas of the Fourth Industrial Revolution*. Available at: https://www.weforum.org/agenda/2017/02/ethics-2-0-how-the-brave-new-world-needs-a-moral-compass/.

Wiley, J. (2009) *Driving Success through Performance Excellence and Employee Engagement*. Online: Kenexa Research Institute. Available at: www.academia.edu/4438802/Driving_Success_Through_PE_and_EE.

Wilson, E. O. (1984) *Biophilia*. Cambridge, MA: Harvard University Press.

Yankelovich, D. and Immerwahr, J. (1984) 'Putting the Work Ethic to Work', *Society*, 21(2), pp. 58–76.

Yerkes, R. and Dodson, J. (1908) 'The Relation of Strength of Stimulus to Rapidity of Habit-Formation', *Journal of Comparative Neurology and Psychology*, 18(1), pp. 459–482.

Zander, M., Hutton, A. and King, L. (2013) 'Exploring Resilience in Paediatric Oncology Nursing Staff', *Collegian*, 20(1), pp. 17–25.

INDEX